A PROMISE OF HOPE—
A CALL TO OBEDIENCE

International Theological Commentary

George A. F. Knight and Frederick Carlson Holmgren
General Editors

A PROMISE OF HOPE—
A CALL TO OBEDIENCE

A Commentary on the Books of

Joel
GRAHAM S. OGDEN

and

Malachi
RICHARD R. DEUTSCH

WM. B. EERDMANS PUBL. CO., GRAND RAPIDS

THE HANDSEL PRESS LTD, EDINBURGH

Copyright © 1987 by Wm. B. Eerdmans Publishing Company

First published 1987 by William B. Eerdmans Publishing Company,
255 Jefferson Ave. S.E., Grand Rapids, Michigan 49503
and
The Handsel Press Limited
33 Montgomery Street, Edinburgh EH7 5JX

Library of Congress Cataloging-in-Publication Data

A Promise of hope — a call to obedience.

(International theological commentary)
Includes bibliographies.
Contents: Restoring the years / Graham S. Ogden —
Calling God's people to obedience / Richard R. Deutsch.
1. Bible. O.T. Joel — Commentaries.
2. Bible. O.T. Malachi — Commentaries.
I. Ogden, Graham S., 1938-   . Restoring the years.   1987.
II. Deutsch, Richard R. Calling God's people to obedience.   1987.
III. Title. IV. Series.
BS1575.3.P76   1987   224'.707   87-19935

Eerdmans ISBN 0-8028-0093-9

British Library Cataloguing in Publication Data

Ogden, Graham S.
A promise of hope, a call to obedience :
a commentary on the Books of Joel and Malachi.
— (International theological commentary).
1. Bible. O.T. Joel — Commentaries
2. Bible. O.T. Malachi — Commentaries
I. Title II. Deutsch, Richard III. Series
224'.707   BS1575.3

Handsel ISBN 0 905312 70 8

CONTENTS

ABBREVIATIONS

ANEP	*The Ancient Near East in Pictures*, ed. J. B. Pritchard, 2nd ed. (Princeton: Princeton University Press, 1969)
ANET	*Ancient Near Eastern Texts Relating to the Old Testament*, ed. J. B. Pritchard, 3rd ed. (Princeton: Princeton University Press, 1969)
ATD	Das Alte Testament Deutsch
BHS	*Biblia Hebraica Stuttgartensia*
ca.	circa (about)
CML	*Canaanite Myths and Legends*, by G. R. Driver (Edinburgh: T. & T. Clark, 1956)
Heb.	Hebrew
IDB	*Interpreter's Dictionary of the Bible*, ed. G. A. Buttrick, et al. 4 vols. (Nashville: Abingdon, 1962)
JB	Jerusalem Bible
JBL	*Journal of Biblical Literature*
KAT	Kommentar zum Alten Testament
LXX	Septuagint
mg	marginal note to the text of the RSV, NEB
MT	Masoretic Text
NEB	New English Bible
NT	New Testament
OT	Old Testament
1QH	*Hodayot* (hymns) from Qumran Cave 1
par.	parallel(s)
RSV	Revised Standard Version
TWAT	*Theologisches Wörterbuch zum Alten Testament*, ed. G. J. Botterweck, et al. (Stuttgart: Kohlhammer, 1970-)
VT	*Vetus Testamentum*
VTSup	*Vetus Testamentum*, Supplements
ZAW	*Zeitschrift für die alttestamentliche Wissenschaft*

EDITORS' PREFACE

The Old Testament alive in the Church: this is the goal of the *International Theological Commentary*. Arising out of changing, unsettled times, this Scripture speaks with an authentic voice to our own troubled world. It witnesses to God's ongoing purpose and to his caring presence in the universe without ignoring those experiences of life that cause one to question his existence and love. This commentary series is written by front-rank scholars who treasure the life of faith.

Addressed to ministers and Christian educators, the *International Theological Commentary* moves beyond the usual critical-historical approach to the Bible and offers a *theological* interpretation of the Hebrew text. Thus, engaging larger textual units of the biblical writings, the authors of these volumes assist the reader in the appreciation of the theology underlying the text as well as its place in the thought of the Hebrew Scriptures. But more, since the Bible is the book of the believing community, its text has acquired ever more meaning through an ongoing interpretation. This growth of interpretation may be found both within the Bible itself and in the continuing scholarship of the Church.

Contributors to the *International Theological Commentary* are Christians — persons who affirm the witness of the New Testament concerning Jesus Christ. For Christians, the Bible is *one* scripture containing the Old and New Testaments. For this reason, a commentary on the Old Testament may not ignore the second part of the canon, namely, the New Testament.

Since its beginning, the Church has recognized a special relationship between the two Testaments. But the precise character of this bond has been difficult to define. Thousands of books and articles have discussed the issue. The diversity of views represented in these publications makes us aware that the Church is not of one mind in expressing the "how" of this relationship. The authors of this commentary share a developing consensus that any serious explanation of the Old Testament's relationship to the New will uphold the integrity of the Old Testament. Even though Christianity is rooted in the soil of the Hebrew Scriptures, the biblical interpreter must take care lest he "christianize" these Scriptures.

Authors writing in this commentary will, no doubt, hold varied views concerning *how* the Old Testament relates to the New. No attempt has been made to dictate one viewpoint in this matter. With the whole Church, we are convinced that the relationship between the two Testaments is real and substantial. But we recognize also the diversity of opinions among Christian scholars when they attempt to articulate fully the nature of this relationship.

In addition to the Christian Church, there exists another people for whom the Old Testament is important, namely, the Jewish community. Both Jews and Christians claim the Hebrew Bible as Scripture. Jews believe that the basic teachings of this Scripture point toward, and are developed by, the Talmud, which assumed its present form about A.D. 500. On the other hand, Christians hold that the Old Testament finds its fulfillment in the New Testament. The Hebrew Bible, therefore, belongs to both the Church and the Synagogue.

Recent studies have demonstrated how profoundly early Christianity reflects a Jewish character. This fact is not surprising because the Christian movement arose out of the context of first-century Judaism. Further, Jesus himself was Jewish, as were the first Christians. It is to be expected, therefore, that Jewish and Christian interpretations of the Hebrew Bible will reveal similarities *and* disparities. Such is the case. The authors of the *International Theological Commentary* will refer to the various Jewish traditions that they consider important for an appreciation of the Old Testament text. Such references will enrich our understanding of certain biblical passages and, as an extra gift, offer us insight into the relationship of Judaism to early Christianity.

An important second aspect of the present series is its *international* character. In the past, Western church leaders were considered to be *the* leaders of the Church — at least by those living in the West! The theology and biblical exegesis done by these scholars dominated the thinking of the Church. Most commentaries were produced in the Western world and reflected the lifestyle, needs, and thoughts of its civilization. But the Christian Church is a worldwide community. People who belong to this universal Church reflect differing thoughts, needs, and lifestyles.

Today the fastest growing churches in the world are to be found, not in the West, but in Africa, Indonesia, South America,

Korea, Taiwan, and elsewhere. By the end of this century, Christians in these areas will outnumber those who live in the West. In our age, especially, a commentary on the Bible must transcend the parochialism of Western civilization and be sensitive to issues that are the special problems of persons who live outside of the "Christian" West, issues such as race relations, personal survival and fulfillment, liberation, revolution, famine, tyranny, disease, war, the poor, religion and state. Inspired of God, the authors of the Old Testament knew what life is like on the edge of existence. They addressed themselves to everyday people who often faced more than everyday problems. Refusing to limit God to the "spiritual," they portrayed him as one who heard and knew the cries of people in pain (see Exod. 3:7-8). The contributors to the *International Theological Commentary* are persons who prize the writings of these biblical authors as a word of life to our world today. They read the Hebrew Scriptures in the twin contexts of ancient Israel and our modern day.

The scholars selected as contributors underscore the international aspect of the series. Representing very different geographical, ideological, and ecclesiastical backgrounds, they come from over seventeen countries. Besides scholars from such traditional countries as England, Scotland, France, Italy, Switzerland, Canada, New Zealand, Australia, South Africa, and the United States, contributors from the following places are included: Israel, Indonesia, India, Thailand, Singapore, Taiwan, and countries of Eastern Europe. Such diversity makes for richness of thought. Christian scholars living in Buddhist, Muslim, or Socialist lands may be able to offer the World Church insights into the biblical message—insights to which the scholarship of the West could be blind.

The proclamation of the biblical message is the focal concern of the *International Theological Commentary*. Generally speaking, the authors of these commentaries value the historical-critical studies of past scholars, but they are convinced that these studies by themselves are not enough. The Bible is more than an object of critical study; it is the revelation of God. In the written Word, God has disclosed himself and his will to humankind. Our authors see themselves as servants of the Word which, when rightly received, brings *shalom* to both the individual and the community.

Joel stands in the same general biblical tradition as found in the book of Lamentations and the Lament Psalms. This commentary not only recognizes that fact, it also interprets details of the book in a manner specific to that background, in the hope that its significance for people of faith in today's broken world may be more easily seen and appreciated. Above all, in its final chapter, the theme of God's readiness to deal with the injustice of our world is seen as a reminder of the divine passion for justice which embraces all humanity.

The messages in the book of Malachi all center on the teachings and demands of the Torah. But the "messenger" does not preach the law; rather he continually stresses that belonging to the people of God demands obedience to God's will. Hypocrisy and blatant disregard for God's known will cannot go unpunished. The particular dispute style of the presentation takes up real or anticipated excuses by the people whom the messenger addresses. The very serious background of these pleas is the strong theological conviction of those returning from the Babylonian exile that unless the people as a whole submit to God's will as laid down in the Torah another and terrible catastrophe will destroy God's people for good.

Such a call to be serious about one's faith appears to be timely today again.

GEORGE A. F. KNIGHT
FREDRICK CARLSON HOLMGREN

RESTORING THE YEARS

A Commentary on the Book of
Joel

GRAHAM S. OGDEN

In Memory
Sydney W. Ogden

CONTENTS

AUTHOR'S PREFACE

During the writing of this small commentary I have been conscious of the Daoist monastery on the mountain opposite, visible from my study, and I have been particularly aware of the distance which separates our two faith worlds. If I am to communicate what my faith means in the context of a society whose religious experience differs so markedly from my own, I must first of all understand how that community perceives itself, its world, and its religious life. Somehow I must build a bridge across the valley. Interpreting the OT calls for a similar venture. Separated as we are historically, geographically, culturally, and linguistically from ancient Israel, we must nevertheless discover a "bridge" across that gap which will facilitate our mutual interaction.

In this brief commentary I have built a "bridge." I have attempted to interpret the book of Joel as much as possible from within the lament tradition to which it purports to belong. I have sought to understand Israel's laments, and I have been appreciative of the many years spent in Asia as a further aid to comprehending a culture in which public lamentation is part of the fabric of life, as it was in ancient Israel. The results of my attempt to bridge the gap between our world and that of Joel are now before the reader, who will detect a number of points at which my interpretation differs from that of other scholars. I have built a bridge, but it is by no means the only bridge. My hope is that it will aid the reader in his or her own attempt to cross over and explore the faith of the community which has left us the book of Joel, a faith refined in the fires of adversity.

It is never possible to thank all of one's mentors, for they are too numerous. However, I would like to pay tribute to three. I wish to thank Dr. Alan Cole, who infected me at an early stage with the notion that the study of the OT could actually be "fun." Dr. Norman Porteous, whose deep interest during my early days of teaching OT in Singapore and since, has been a constant source of ecnouragement. Dr. Bernhard Anderson, whose rare

5

gift of academic excellence combined with genuine pastoral concern for his students, provided a model for the would-be pastor and teacher to emulate. To the series editors, Fredrick Holmgren and George Knight, are due thanks for their attention to detail and the enthusiasm with which they have assisted the production of this commentary. Finally, I would express thanks to my wife, Lois, partner and friend in the life and work of faith.

Taipei
GRAHAM S. OGDEN
EPIPHANY, 1984

INTRODUCTION

Second among the so-called Minor Prophets of Israel stands the prophecy of Joel. Its three chapters (four chapters in Hebrew — 1:1-20; 2:1-27; 3:1-5 [= Eng. 2:28-32]; 4:1-21 [= Eng. 3:1-21]) represent a distinctive document, for, apart from a brief introduction in 1:1, Joel contains few of the marks of prophetic literature. It has none of the usual attacks on the social, religious, and moral failures of the nation, no indictment of its leaders; it employs few of the recognized prophetic forms of address. Little is known about its author and date of composition. For these reasons alone the book is worth our attention.

Understanding Joel is important for another reason. It is a work which reflects a community under threat and in pain, a problem many contemporary Christian communities face. Therefore, the world church may profit from Joel's words as it lives out its faith in a world marked by calamity and injustice. From Joel's words we hear the word of God addressed to the faithful living under tyranny, and in a world in which many have lost hope. To all in such anguish of body, mind, and spirit, God speaks words of reassurance: he is in control and will right society's wrongs.

So let us begin the task of hearing and understanding what this prophet has to say. We start with some technical questions which are important for a fuller grasp of the book.

UNITY

Two basic views have been taken concerning the unity of the book of Joel. The first is that the book consists of two parts, the first half being earlier and by a different author than the second half. This view was first put forward in 1872 by M. Vernes and has been followed with modifications by scholars such as J. Rothstein, Bewer, Duhm, Sellin, T. H. Robinson, Eissfeldt, and Plöger.

The phrase "the day of the LORD" was the basic criterion for this division. The argument was that in the first half of the book the "day" was believed to have already arrived, but in the second half the "day" was a future, or even eschatological, moment.

The second view, that the book is a unity, has always persisted in parallel with the first. For example, in 1926 L. Dennefeld argued against Vernes's thesis, and others such as Jepsen, Kapelrud, J. Thompson, Weiser, H. W. Wolff, Allen, and Ahlström have agreed with Dennefeld's conclusion. Although these other scholars may not have agreed with Dennefeld's method of argument, nevertheless there has been a strong movement in support of his claim that Joel represents a unity. Of the above authors, Wolff has presented the strongest case for the book's unity, and we could say that this is perhaps the dominant view at this moment. Wolff's arguments rest on content, structure, and linguistic connections throughout Joel.

Although Wolff's arguments for the unity of Joel are significant, his viewpoint can be further supported by a more complete listing of the abundance of literary features which Joel uses. These include key words and phrases, inclusions, assonance, thematic associations, and contrasts, and are to be found below in Appendix 1.

STRUCTURE

To define the unity of Joel in terms of authorship or of literary cohesion is to present only one aspect of the issue. The wider question of overall structure helps us further understand the nature of its unity. In general terms, Joel is a literary work based on a lament liturgy, beginning with the Call to Lamentation, followed by Cries of Lament, Yahweh's Response, and reaching a high point with the Promises of Divine Aid as Judah confronts a major crisis.

After the Title in 1:1, there is a Summons to the people (1:2-3) to come and listen to what Joel has to say. This Summons consists of a rhetorical question (1:2b), which emphasizes that Judah's current crisis is unparalleled in the nation's history and that it will be talked about for a long time to come.

The message of the book begins in 1:4 with a statement about the complete devastation brought about by a locust plague. Use of this image in 1:4 and 2:5 serves to bind together the two opening chapters. Within that larger unit we find a number of clearly marked subsections all related to a national lament liturgy. Beginning in 1:5-14 is the Call to Lamentation, followed in 1:15-18 by the first Cry of Lament. This first Cry prefers the pronoun "we," for it is Judah who speaks. In the second Cry of Lament (1:19-20) the pronoun "I," with the corporate meaning "we," is preferred. Both cries speak of the destruction and ensuing hardship endured by man and beast bound in life together. Each Cry has distinctive imagery: 1:15-18 paints a picture of drought; 1:19-20 prefers to speak of fire and flame. These are parallel Cries of Lament. The second chapter opens with two Cries of Alarm, the first of which (2:1-14) is considerably longer than the second (2:15-17). The first Cry of Alarm urges Judah to prepare for the coming crisis (2:1-10), while 2:11-14 is an additional Call to lament and weep. Although the second Cry of Alarm is briefer, it uses the same introductory phrase as 2:1. Prompting the nation to preparation (2:15-16), it then calls their spiritual leaders to lamentation (2:17).

The next major subdivision (2:18-27) presumes that the nation has heeded the Call to Lament, for it presents the Divine Response as a promise, specifically reminding the people of God's faithfulness (2:18-20). It encourages Judah not to be afraid but to rejoice (2:21-23). There follows one further and parallel Divine Response (2:24-27). In both Responses the theme is the same— Yahweh will reverse the destruction caused by the invaders. Furthermore, both Responses draw upon the grain, wine, and oil motif from ch. 1, outlining how Judah will be filled with God's provisions. The nation will never again face the shame they presently know.

As we continue in ch. 2 (ch. 3 in Hebrew), we hear the prophet promise that God will pour out his Spirit at some future moment upon all people (2:28-29). Here Joel expands the preceding Divine Response; at the same time he provides a link with the following oracles concerning foreign nations. This promise is coupled with another promise (2:30-32), which describes cataclysmic events that will precede the deliverance God brings on the "day of the LORD."

In ch. 3 (= Hebrew ch. 4) we find a series of four oracles (vv. 1-3, 4-8, 9-18, 19-21) each carrying a word of judgment against certain foreign nations for their treachery against Judah. In addition to the theme of judgment, they also bring a message of comfort and hope to Judah. Although each oracle is independent in form and general content, they have a common element, namely, that the judgment of the nations will take the form of evil deeds returning on their own heads; they will suffer as they have made Judah to suffer.

9

SETTING

The setting for the book of Joel also helps describe its unity. By this we mean that the lament ritual which forms the book's background is another unifying factor, for the various parts of the book all reflect elements in a lament liturgy. Thus the setting enables us to speak of a unity of function in Joel.

Joel's present form is that of a well-constructed literary work. We may assume that originally each part was even more closely related to the liturgy of lament, but now each has become part of a written document. The lament setting is visible not simply in the several invitations to "lament" and "wail" (1:5, 8, 11, 13, 18), to "put on sackcloth" (1:13), to "sanctify a fast" (1:14), or to "cry to Yahweh" (1:14), which punctuate 1:5-14, but also in this section's imagery, which is most typical of lament psalms. For example, Ps. 57:4 uses the imagery of lions and lions' teeth to describe an attacking nation (cf. Joel 1:6); we read of the destruction of fields in Ps. 79:7; 80:14-16; Lam. 4:9, while invading forces are likened to a fire in Ps. 80:16; 83:14; and Lam. 2:3.

Psalm 79 shows even more clearly that Joel belongs in the lament setting. In this psalm the nations invade God's land, his "inheritance" (79:1; Joel 3:2), and "shed blood" as though it were water (79:3; Joel 3:19). Israel is made a "reproach" by such an invasion (79:4; Joel 2:17) and the foreign troops mockingly call "Where is your God?" (79:10; Joel 2:17).

In addition to its clear connections to prophetic literature, the book of Joel has another and more significant aspect, namely, its setting in lamentation.

INTERPRETATION

If we are unclear about the setting of this or any other OT book, we risk interpreting it in ways inconsistent with that setting, and thus may distort its meaning.

In what follows, we will take seriously the lament setting from which Joel comes. This approach will have several implications for our interpretation. But first some brief comments about laments in the OT are necessary.

The term *lament* in English has a negative connotation; it usually suggests a complaining, whining spirit. But the term as applied to OT laments needs to be qualified, for those psalms classified as laments almost always climax on a positive note with the worshiper confessing abiding confidence in God. The lament's final tone is one of faith; it expresses confidence that the outcome lies in the hands of God, who is compassionate and faithful. From this vantage point we see that the "lament" is actually a plea for God to come to the aid of those who maintain unswerving trust in him despite the trials of the moment. Between the complaint section and the final vow of thanksgiving there was an opportunity for the priest or officiant to speak words of assurance to the suppliant. This reminder that God had not abandoned his people could take various forms, but in the case of a national cry for help, it would logically be a statement of God's judgment on the foreign power who was responsible for the present calamity.

What are some of the features of OT laments?

1. Laments traditionally use stylized or generalized language. Numerous unrelated images used together may describe one situation. For example, bulls, dogs, and evildoers in Ps. 22 are all terms describing the people's "enemies." Such usage is not to be understood in a literal manner. As we look at Joel 1 we note that three different images describe the problem confronting Judah — a locust plague, a drought, and fire. From what we know of lament language we may assert that none of these images expresses the actual situation being faced; rather, each one vividly portrays that a crisis is at hand.

2. Laments generally, though not exclusively, are cries for God's deliverance from what the speaker sees as undeserved calamity (Ps. 17:3-5; 26:1-3; 35:7; 44:17-22; 59:3-4). Israel's enemies are spoken of as unjust and evil, as having caused Israel's pain because of their contempt for Yahweh and his people. It is important to recognize this characteristic of the lament. Most laments do not contain any plea for forgiveness because the problem of the moment is not Israel's sin but the inhumanity and evil of others toward Israel (cf. Pss. 17, 26).

From this vantage point we can understand why Joel does not condemn Judah for its injustice and vile behavior. Unlike other prophets, Joel does not mention Judah's departure from God's standards. In fact, 2:23 and 3:19 give the distinct impression that Judah is innocent. This is what we would expect in a lament setting.

In view of these two factors — the lament's plea of innocence and Joel's silence about Judah's sin — we conclude that Judah does not need to "repent." The crisis of the moment cannot be interpreted as divine judgment falling on a sinful Judah. Therefore, when Joel urges the people to "turn to God" (2:12-14) he simply means they should turn to him for assistance in meeting the present crisis. We should not assume that "turn" means "repent," even though it has that meaning in other prophetic works, such as Jeremiah.

3. National laments in the Psalms are liturgical responses to threats which the nation faces. Although these crises may be of varying kinds, most of them are attacks by foreign powers. In the case of Joel, evidence that Judah faces just such a crisis is found in 1:5-6 and 2:2. The identity of the nation which threatens Judah on this occasion is not given immediately.

In Joel's Call to Lamentation, in the Cries of Alarm, or in other portions of the liturgy, it is unwise to search for historical references. In the past, references to the "wall" (2:7, 9), "city" (2:9), and such have been interpreted as evidence that the walls of Jerusalem had been rebuilt following Judah's return from the Exile. In principle, however, this is misguided. Other national laments use the same general terms, and it is apparent that they denote an attack on the nation as a whole rather than being specific landmarks.

4. The foreign nation oracles of ch. 3 are also part of the lament liturgy. Each of these oracles represents the prophet's response to the people's cry for divine aid. For this reason we conclude that ch. 3 is not concerned with eschatological events but with the impending judgment against Judah's enemies, a judgment for which Judah pleads in the lament itself (2:17).

LANGUAGE

Joel has many connections with prophetic as well as lament literature, and so both influences are found in its language.

One of the most intriguing features of Joel is its extensive quotation of other prophetic writings. We may generally state that where such parallels exist it is Joel who has done the borrowing (Wolff, *Joel,* 5, 10). The reason for this conclusion is that Joel places those materials within his own particular expressions. For example, Joel incorporates 2:13-14, which echo thoughts from Jonah 3:9 and 4:2, into a section carrying his basic "before and after" theme. Sometimes Joel turns the borrowed statement around — 2:3b reverses Isa. 51:3; 2:21 similarly treats Ps. 126:3; 3:10 reverses Isa. 2:4. Virtually all of Joel's quotations come from other prophets, and the list is quite extensive (see Appendix 2). That these other materials were known to Joel helps us date his work.

AUTHORSHIP AND DATE

What we know about Joel the prophet can be inferred only from within the book itself. We have no independent evidence about him. We assume that Joel was a prophet from Judah with special ties to the nation's cultic activities. Although he apparently was not a priest (cf. 1:13 and 2:17, in which he appears to distance himself deliberately from the priestly group), he was familiar at least with the lament liturgy and participated in it.

As far as the date of the book is concerned, scholars have depended on allusions within, but these by nature are open to various interpretations, so it has been difficult to be precise. We may illustrate the problem by considering 3:19 and the references to Edom and Egypt. If we assume that this incident refers to Shishak's invasions of Judah during Rehoboam's reign (1 Kgs. 14:25-26) and that Edom's revolt is a revolt against Jehoram (2 Kgs. 8:20-22), then Joel must be dated near the 9th cent. B.C. It is also possible that the reference to Edom is to its participation in Babylon's attack on Judah in 587 B.C. On this basis, Joel is an exilic or early postexilic work.

Many scholars today accept a postexilic date for Joel. Some suggest a date as late as the 4th cent. B.C. (Wolff, *Joel*, 5), others as early as the 6th cent. B.C. (Allen, *Joel*, 24). The latter view emphasizes the references to the alliance of Tyre and the Philistine city of Ashkelon (3:4), and the references to Greek traders (3:6) and Sabeans (3:8). It is argued that trading relations between these groups are possible during the late 6th cent. B.C. The former view, that Joel is as late as the early 4th cent., is based largely on the belief that 1:9, 14 speak of the temple, and 2:7, 9 refer to the *wall* of Jerusalem. The argument runs that these could not have been completed until the time of Nehemiah, that is, ca. 445 B.C. Wolff further argues that 3:4 implies a coastal alliance during the Persian period, and that in Joel's time Judah was ruled as a theocracy by "priests" and "ministers" (1:2, 13-14; 2:16-17). This would place Joel after Ezra and Nehemiah.

Literary evidence such as the use of quotations from other prophets would date Joel later than Deutero-Isaiah, Obadiah, and Malachi, that is, during the early postexilic period.

For reasons already given, this author believes that we should not attempt to date Joel on the basis of terms such as the "wall" or the "house of your God." That the "wall" is Jerusalem's wall is deliberately unclear. To so identify it, or to go so far as to equate it with the wall repaired by Nehemiah, is unwarranted. The "house of God" (1:13, 14, 16) is a way of referring to a sanctuary, and is not to be construed as evidence that the temple had been rebuilt. In Ps. 55:9-11 and 59:6, 14 there are similar references to "city," "wall," and "market place." These are general terms rather than features of the city of Jerusalem.

The only point at which we may expect historical references is in ch. 3, the place at which the liturgy itself becomes specific. Oracles of judgment against foreign nations are Joel's responses to those several occasions on which Judah lamented in face of particular threats to its welfare. When speaking of the date of Joel we are actually speaking of the span of time during that early postexilic period when the liturgy was used and reused.

On the basis of arguments in the exegesis which follows, this author believes that each foreign nation oracle refers to events surrounding the Babylonian attacks on Jerusalem that led to the latter's destruction in 587 B.C. Upon their return to Jerusalem in 538 and after, the returnees had to confront the devastation and ruin of their homeland. The despair and hardship of those early days in Jerusalem are well-known, and although fifty years had passed since Babylon had razed it, Judah still felt the pain of those days as intensely as if it were yesterday. Their grief was poured out in lamentation.

The tenor of the oracles and the many connections with Obadiah indicate that the laments of the returnees were frequent and bitter. Judah longed that those who brought about the destruction of Jerusalem, whose ruins were once again before their eyes, be duly punished. Joel assures them that it will be so, that Judah's present misery will be avenged.

Thus we conclude that Joel reflects and records material from the lament liturgies of those early days after the return to Jerusalem, the late 6th cent. B.C., a little later than Obadiah.

JOEL AS THEOLOGIAN

If we know something of the basic position from which an author looks at life, it helps us understand his or her message. This applies to all kinds of literature, and certainly to the OT prophetic writings.

As we approach the book of Joel, being aware of some of his central ideas enables us to appreciate better what he says and the way in which he expresses himself.

1. *Joel and the Davidic Covenant.* Joel's theological starting point is in the Davidic covenant tradition. That is, he understands the

relationship between Yahweh and Judah in terms of an eternal covenant entered into with the house of David (see 2 Sam. 7; Ps. 89). Zion and its temple are visible signs of this covenant. In Judah this was probably the dominant view. In the foreign nation oracles (Joel 3) Zion is spoken of as the place where Yahweh resides and as the source of future blessing; it is also the place of judgment. That Judah's future will be assured *for ever* (3:20) is a thought which belongs to this tradition. Joel confirms that Judah will have this bright future because they are "his people"; no conditions are attached to the granting of Yahweh's aid.

2. *Yahweh Is Lord of History.* The full sweep of world events, the rise and fall of nations, lies within Yahweh's care and control. Avenging wrong and bringing blessing are the categories most used to speak of Yahweh's action, and such action is not limited to Judah alone. These acts are part of Yahweh's universal work. The "day of Yahweh" can be any moment in history in which Yahweh's action is carried out. In Joel, "the day" is the time for judging the nations and for bringing blessing and deliverance to Judah.

3. *Yahweh Is Judge.* Joel pays special attention to Yahweh as the one who upholds justice. The lament literature evidences a deep concern with Yahweh's role as the defender of those who trust in him. So too in Joel we discover that God will punish evil wherever it is committed. This theme we find in other prophets, such as Amos (cf. Amos 1 – 2). Frequently, historical events are the means God uses to carry out his judgments, but in Joel the emphasis is on what *Yahweh* does, as though it were almost independent of human effort. Perhaps this is a healthy reminder to those who stress the human element in the struggle for justice and peace, that ultimately we need to rely on Yahweh (see the Excursus).

4. *Yahweh's Actions Have a Purpose.* In 2:27 and 3:17 Joel declares that Yahweh's actions have a determined purpose, namely, to make Yahweh known. Whether in judgment or in blessing, the character of God is visible and knowable. Although Joel shares this view with other writers, such as Deutero-Isaiah (see Isa. 45:3, 4, 6), he does appear to limit this revelational possibility to Judah. In doing so he shows a narrower attitude than does Deutero-Isaiah or Ezekiel, for whom God's actions are for all nations to see. This difference may stem from Joel's specific purpose; he is seeking to bring comfort to Judah.

5. *Joel and Worship.* Worship, or the cult, is clearly important to Joel. He is a prophet whose ministry is that of bringing God's word to a nation in grief. Their plea for help is expressed through

the formal worship of the lament ritual, and in that same liturgy Judah hears God's words of assurance and comfort. For Joel, worship is the vehicle by which the prophet conveys to God's people Yahweh's compassion for all who are dismayed and oppressed.

THE CHRISTIAN AND LAMENTATION

Lamentation was an important element in Judah's liturgical life. This is evidenced by the large number of laments, both national and individual, preserved in the book of Psalms. However, lament rituals similar to those in which such psalms found expression are not prominent in Christian tradition. How, then, might Christians respond to the message of Joel?

In his article "The Role of the Lament in the Theology of the Old Testament" (*Interpretation* 28 [1974] 20-38), C. Westermann reminds us that Israel's cry of distress is inextricably linked with its experiences of salvation (cf. Exod. 3:7-9). Thus salvation has, as its forerunner, the plea for divine aid in the midst of crisis. The relationship of the cry of distress to the experience of God's salvation, while not unique to Israel, lies at the very heart of biblical theology.

When we consider the central liturgical drama of the Christian tradition, the celebration of Christ's death and resurrection, we, like Israel, are celebrating our deliverance from "bondage." The same may be said of Christian preaching and social commitment, for all ultimately have to do with deliverance and the restoration to wholeness, individually and corporately, with God and our neighbor.

While as Christians we emphasize the saving love of God, we have little opportunity liturgically to pour out our fears, pain, anger, and frustrations, or our doubts about God's care. This is not to say that opportunities to confess sin and our need for deliverance are absent, for they are certainly built into our liturgies. However, they are usually more restrained and tend to focus on confessing sin. As such they have a different purpose and emphasis from the OT laments, for the latter generally have no call for repentance. What Christians need liturgically is a mechanism for the release of other emotions and concerns we have, as well as opportunities to hear God's word of comfort and assurance that he has not abandoned us to an uncaring world. To lament or pour out one's despair in a context of worship is appropriate, for there we call upon a compassionate God to act

16

against the powers that bind us. There too we hear the assurance of God's commitment to all in need, whatever that need may be, and we are able to move from the cry for help to thanksgiving for anticipated deliverance.

Laments in the OT, as honest outpourings of the people's responses to crises, marked the beginning of the healing process. If our liturgical life is to have its fullest possible impact on our spiritual pilgrimages, we have to learn from the book of Joel. The healing of broken relationships, of social chaos, of spiritual doubts and fears, begins with an unrestrained expression before God of those deep feelings we have about what is threatening us. To be able to do so as part of our liturgies of salvation will heighten their significance for us by bringing the compassion of God into direct contact with those matters which deeply trouble us.

CHAPTER 1

THE DEVASTATION OF THE LAND

EDITORIAL INTRODUCTION (1:1)

Joel here uses a standard expression found in several other prophetic books — Hosea, Micah, and Zephaniah. Unlike some, such as Amos, Isaiah, or Ezekiel, there is no mention of the time at which Joel prophesied, so we know nothing more about him than that his father's name was Pethuel. While the name Joel occurs frequently in the OT (1 Sam. 8:2; 1 Chron. 5:12; 7:3; Ezra 10:43; etc.), Pethuel is not found elsewhere. "Joel" means "Yahweh is God," but the meaning of his father's name is not clear.

Joel appears to have lived in Jerusalem; he was a prophet familiar with the cultic life of Judah, although not himself a priest.

THE ADDRESS (1:2-3)

Joel's first words are addressed to the leaders and people. The call to "hear" is frequently used by prophets to arouse the people's interest (cf. Isa. 42:18; Amos 8:4; Mic. 3:1, 9). To address the nation's elders rather than the king is consistent with a postexilic date for the book, a time when Judah no longer was ruled by a monarch. However, elders were important in Israel's social pattern from as early as Mosaic times (Exod. 19:7).

Joel begins with an address in parallel form: "hear" and "give ear"; "elders" and "all who live in the land." Such parallel phrases are typical of prophetic and poetic writing.

The question which follows in v. 2b is a rhetorical question expecting the answer no. By this means Joel emphasizes the uniqueness of the present moment. Such a calamity has never been known before, and it will be talked about well into the future (v. 3). Joel's point is that this is an unprecedented crisis which will leave an indelible impression on the nation's memory.

INTRODUCTION TO THE CALL TO LAMENTATION (1:4)

The voracious appetite of four kinds of locust, or perhaps of four different stages in the locust life cycle, are used to form a highly descriptive expression for complete devastation — nothing remains after they sweep by.

The three parallel lines of this verse are a bald statement, the content of which is independent of vv. 2-3 and v. 5, and the verse has all the flavor of a traditional aphorism. This, together with a reference to all four locusts again in 2:25, suggests that 1:4 has an important role in introducing the Call to Lamentation. It is also the first element in the inclusion (1:4 and 2:25) which binds together chs. 1 and 2. The locust imagery is not a description of an actual locust plague, but is one of three different images in these chapters (see the section on "Interpretation" in the Introduction above), the others being drought (1:9-12, 13, 17-18) and fire (1:19-20; 2:3). All refer to the destruction which Judah sees all around it. The use of several images to describe one event is typical of laments. In Ps. 69, threatened drowning and libelous attacks from enemies are used; in Ps. 22 the psalmist is mocked by enemies and is attacked by bulls, lions, dogs, wild oxen, and the sword. Each expression is an image only. Although they seem to be inappropriate together, this kind of multiple imagery is found in all laments.

CALL TO LAMENTATION (1:5-14)

This section is marked by a series of imperatives with attached motive clauses, an arrangement which breaks the section into five segments — vv. 5-7, 8-10, 11-12, 13, 14. The first of these calls Judah to awake to the reality of the present calamity, for a powerful enemy has invaded and brought such destruction that nothing remains (cf. v. 4). The following three segments (vv. 8-10, 11-12, 13) urge formal lamentation, each imperative having similar motivation, namely, a shortage of food caused by the enemy's invasion. The fifth and final segment, v. 14, reiterates the Call to Lament addressed to the nation and its leaders (1:2).

5-7   Having no wine to drink or to offer sacrificially is a theme found in four of the five segments of the Call to Lament. "Drunkards" and "drinkers of wine" (v. 5) are parallel terms, and are therefore not necessarily terms of disparagement. They convey the idea of those who enjoy wine. A shortage of wine is grounds for the call to "weep" and "wail." "Sweet wine" is the term for the juice of the freshly trodden grape, the first stage in the wine-making process. If this is cut off, then there will be no wine for later enjoyment — hence the lamentation.

The motive clause of this segment follows in v. 6 and refers to an army of vast proportions having swept across the land, in numbers and destructive power like the proverbial locust. The invading nation — Heb. *goy* describes any non-Israelite person — is the reality (cf. ch. 3) whose power is compared to that of the fierce lion and lioness. "Teeth" and "fangs" are used in parallel in Job 29:17; Ps. 58:6; and Prov. 30:14, but often in the laments the lion and its powerful jaws are apt descriptions of an enemy (Ps. 7:2; 10:9; 17:12; 57:4). The enemy nation has "come up against" Judah, which Joel, as God's representative, describes as his own land. This attitude to the land prompts God's response in 2:18 — because it is "his land" he comes to its aid when it is threatened.

Specifically, in v. 7 the invading army destroyed the "vines" and "fig trees" (cf. 2:22), two terms for the bountiful production of the land. The breaking down and stripping of vines and trees leaves behind nothing but a scene of devastation (RSV "waste," Heb. *shammah*). This term conveys the gravity of the present crisis facing Judah, for the nation's very life is at stake.

The appropriateness of the locust imagery and its function in 1:4 and 2:25 are immediately clear. It represents vast numbers and complete destruction, wholly applicable to the invading armies as they forged their way toward Jerusalem.

8-10 Wailing publicly, dressed in coarse sackcloth, is a common Eastern or oriental way of expressing grief, though perhaps today confined mostly to funeral rites. Joel calls upon the people to wail with an intensity similar to the deep rending cry of a young girl whose betrothed dies suddenly before the wedding. The expression "husband of her youth," which does not occur elsewhere in the OT, describes the young man who has been legally betrothed to the girl in question, and whom she is preparing to wed (cf. Mal. 2:14, "wife of your youth"). Just prior to the wedding he dies, and with him her hopes for the future. The special verb for "lament," *'eli*, is used only here in the OT.

Cereal grains and wine were two of the many elements offered sacrificially (Lev. 23:18). Judah faces a situation in which supplies of both are cut off, meaning that sacrificial rituals which expressed the relationship between Judah and Yahweh were no longer possible. So the priests mourn. The people are urged to join them in mourning the loss of the symbols of God's blessing and their own tokens of devotion.

Not only do the priests mourn, but the land itself joins them in lamenting what has happened to it. This situation is dramatized by the alliteration — the "fields" *(sadeh)* are "laid waste" *(shadad)*. Then comes the motive clause for this segment (v. 10). The nation is called to lament because its basic provisions are taken away — grain, wine, and oil have ceased. The use of three verbs for destruction in so brief a sentence is a way of drawing vivid attention to the ruin of the land. Whether the calamity is caused by marauding troops, as in vv. 6-7, or by drought cannot be determined on the basis of these brief statements, nor is it necessary to be specific in the lament context.

11-12   A double call for lamentation opens this segment, which is marked by an interesting wordplay — "be confounded" *(hobishu)* and "wither" *(yabeshu)*. Farmers and those who till the soil are addressed. The motive for their lamentation is the loss of the harvest and the fruitlessness of their labor.

Various fruit trees have been affected (v. 12) with the result that there are no more grapes, figs, pomegranates, dates, or apples. Twofold use of the verb "wither" *(yabesh)* makes it certain that the harvest failure is caused by drought rather than enemy troops or "locusts" invading. A second motive clause (v. 12b) gives the reason for lamentation — the "drought" of joy in the community. The background for this thought is the celebration in the fields that traditionally marks the close of the harvest (cf. Deut. 16:13). Drought is used here metaphorically as a second image for the present calamity alongside that of the locusts.

13   We return to the theme of the shortage of grain and wine for offerings (cf. vv. 8-10) and to the call to the clergy to take off their festal robes and in their place to don the rough sackcloth used as mourning dress. Four imperatives call them to institute the lament ritual (cf. 1 Kgs. 21:27; Jer. 4:8), the vigil in which the nation's pain is poured out. This time the motive for lament is given as the withholding of sacrificial gifts from the temple or sanctuary. Whether they are deliberately "withheld" *(mana')* because of the shortage of food or for some other reason, such as destruction by invaders or drought, is unclear. However, lacking the elements for an offering to God, the priests are to lead the nation in pleading for divine intervention to end the present calamity.

14   The final segment and climax of the Call to Lamentation is
addressed to the elders and people (cf. 1:2). It uses traditional
language — "Sanctify a fast, call a solemn assembly. Gather . . .
and cry to the LORD" (cf. 2:16; 3:9; 2 Kgs. 10:20; etc.). What
purpose did lamenting serve? Essentially it was a ritual allowing
the individual or group to express its deep anguish over what had
taken place or was currently happening. In Joel a national crisis,
an invasion of enemy troops, prompted the lament. A profoundly
religious act, lamenting in Israel involved dressing in sackcloth,
fasting, and gathering to sing lament songs as a plea for God's
assistance. The verb *za'aq,* "cry," carries a very emotional tone
and depicts a person calling for help and deliverance from a most
agonizing situation. Words of comfort and assurance as a response to the plea, spoken by the priest or prophet officiating as
God's spokesman, concluded the liturgy.

Joel 1:5-14 calls Judah to plead publicly for Yahweh's help. We
note references to locusts, invading armies, and drought, woven
into a theme of destruction of crops. In the context of lamentation,
the locust plague and drought paint a picture of complete devastation of the land. There is no reference to Judah's sins, no
indictment of the nation, so we assume that the lament is not an
act of penitence but a plea for help (see further on 2:12-14). The
crisis is nowhere spoken of as punishment for the nation's disobedience; rather, it is a deeply distressing fact of life which Judah
longs to have corrected. This is fully understandable if we recognize that the lament is offered when the people of Judah have
returned from Babylon to Jerusalem after having paid the price
for their earlier errors. What they are lamenting now is the fact
that the land is so devastated that there is no food.

Public lamentation in Judah appears to have been a frequent
practice if we take account of the number of laments, both individual and corporate, in the book of Psalms. Joel 1:5-14 is one
example of the Call to Lamentation; we presume that similar calls
regularly preceded the liturgy in which the lament was sung (cf.
2 Sam. 3:21; 1 Kgs. 21:8-9; Jonah 3:6-9; etc.). Priest, prophet, or
king could initiate the Call. Based on a belief in God's unswerving
commitment to his people and his land (cf. Joel 2:18-19), Israel
turned to God as the ultimate source of deliverance from all crises
(see 2:30-32). No problem lies outside his care, and out of such
life-threatening situations God can and will bring new life.

From the example of the Call we have just considered in Joel
1, we note several formal features: (1) imperatives urging people

to participate in the ritual; (2) mention of those addressed by the Call; (3) a motive clause introduced by "for" (*ki* or *ʿal*).

Joel's Call to Lamentation is perhaps the most comprehensive example of such a Call in the OT.

CRY OF LAMENT, I (1:15-18)

An account of the crisis faced by the people forms a central part of each lament psalm (see Ps. 79:1-4; 83:2-5; etc.), and Joel 1:15-18 conforms to this pattern. It begins with an unusual cry of terror (*ʾahah*), a cry found in laments, but generally in the form "Alas, my Lord Yahweh" (cf. Josh. 7:7; Judg. 6:22; Jer. 1:6; 4:10). The example in Joel 1:15 is identical with Ezek. 30:2, "Alas for the day." What is this "day"? From the standpoint of the lament context we conclude that the "day" is simply "today," the moment of present crisis. It differs from the "day of Yahweh" because the latter is yet to come (cf. Isa. 13:6; Ezek. 30:3; Obad. 15; Zeph. 1:7).

The "day of Yahweh" is a concept used five times in Joel (1:15; 2:1, 11, 31; 3:14) but only sixteen times in the entire OT, although other related terms do appear more frequently. Typically, the phrase is used in oracles against Israel and Judah or against foreign nations, and describes that moment or event when Yahweh acts in judgment or salvation. It is Yahweh's day, because he is the one who acts. The object of that action may be Israel, Judah, or the nations, but the prophets warn that in the near future Yahweh will carry out his sentence on those who have offended against his justice. To oppressed peoples everywhere, this is "good news."

In v. 15 Judah's cry expressed its fear—it interprets today's crisis as a sign that the day of God's judgment (*shod mishshadday*) is on its way. The use of "Almighty" (*shadday*) is interesting, for it is the divine name of ancient times (cf. Gen. 17:1) and also of hymnic usage (cf. Ps. 91:1). Here it is used because it sounds similar to the word for "ruin" (*shod*). The ruin of their land, Judah believed, signified the beginning of greater destruction, so they voiced their terror in lament form. That such fear was misguided is the conclusion we draw from Joel's oracles of comfort and the inappropriateness of repentance. According to the prophetic words of consolation, Judah need fear no additional devastations, at least not at this time. We see this view also in the way in which "the day of Yahweh" in 2:31 and 3:14 refers to a time of judgment not for Judah but for the nations who have caused this predicament; the continuing threat of judgment which hung over Judah and which "the day" expresses has been applied to Judah's enemies.

Thus we detect two uses of "the day of the LORD" concept in this book. The first, the idea that the "day" will signal a time of judgment, is present in 1:15-18. The second, that the "day" will be one of salvation for God's people, is that which we note in the later chapters (cf. 2:30-32). It is this second use that is important in the message of comfort which Joel brings to a disconsolate Judah.

The question asked in v. 16 is actually a way of stating forcefully that "food" supplies and "joy" have been cut off. We have already met these ideas in vv. 9, 12. This verse explains why Judah believed that the "day of Yahweh," as a time of judgment against them, was approaching. According to Deuteronomy and its tradition, a bountiful harvest was one proof of God's favor and was cause for rejoicing (see Deut. 12:7; 26:10, 11). From this point of view, we may understand how the failure of the crops could be construed as evidence of God's blessing having been withdrawn and of judgment approaching.

Drought is again used in v. 17 as a metaphor for the present calamity (cf. 1:2). One problem with knowing precisely what this verse means is that several words in the first line occur only here in the OT, and their meaning is debated (see RSV mg). The general context, however, suggests that the seed grain planted has not germinated and grown due to lack of moisture. The storage places prepared for the grain expected at harvest time have been broken down *(nehersu)*, presumably by the invading army (cf. 1:6). The final clause of v. 17, "because the grain has failed," raises a slight difficulty, for the failure of the crop would hardly cause the storage bins to collapse. It is best to see the phrase referring back to v. 16—food and joy are cut off because the crop has failed.

As the description of the calamity continues (v. 18), the "cattle" and "sheep" are said to join in the lament. They too have nothing to eat; destruction of crops and pasture is total.

CRY OF LAMENT, II (1:19-20)

This second Cry of Lament is more personal. The suppliant turns to Yahweh with his plea (cf. Ps. 28:1; 30:8). As he portrays the crisis the key word is *fire;* observe the refrain, "fire has devoured the pastures of the wilderness" (vv. 19, 20). The destruction of "all the trees of the field" is a theme already used in 1:12, and the notion that animals join the lament echoes 1:18. The verb "dry up" we noted in 1:12. Thus key themes in the Cry respond to those in the Call to Lamentation (1:5-14), but with one difference, namely, the introduction of a significant new metaphor — that of fire (cf. Ps. 74:7; 118:12). Fire constitutes the third image Joel uses to describe the invading army and the destruction it brought with it. Verse 20 preserves the image of drought (cf. v. 17). Man and beast together plead for Yahweh's intervention. In ch. 1, then, with its Call to Lamentation and Cries of Lament, Joel has used one theme throughout — the destruction of the land's productivity — but expressed that theme under a variety of metaphors.

CHAPTER 2

BEFORE AND AFTER

CRY OF ALARM, I (2:1-14)

This first Cry of Alarm opens with three imperatives summoning Judah to prepare to meet the invading army. Judah is warned that the "day" is near and that it will be a frightening event, for the awesome power of God will be displayed on the stage of history. From a literary point of view, the *day* is a central concept (2:1, 2, 11) which helps us define the extent of this unit.

The next subsection (2:2b-10) has three major literary or rhetorical features: (1) a series of metaphors likening the invading army to a number of different and fearful phenomena; (2) the contrast "before and after" (2:2b, 3, 6, 10, 11), which also serves as a marker for smaller divisions beginning at vv. 3, 6, 10, 11; (3) the use of key words and of special vocabulary.

In this unit, key words are especially important, particularly words describing the invading nation. In v. 2 the enemy is spoken of as "great" *(rab)* and "powerful" *('atsum)*. This powerful nation is mentioned again in v. 5. Several words relating to fire *('esh, lahab, 'akalah)* dominate vv. 3 and 5, while in both vv. 7 and 9 enemy troops are described as running headlong forward, and as climbing over the walls in their advance across the land.

Joel writes here as though the enemy is presently invading Judah. However, in doing this, he is in fact using a superb literary device — he pictures the invasion of 587 some fifty years before, and projects it into the present, as he calls the nation to seek God's help.

The third subsection (2:11-14) describes Yahweh's power and the sound that goes before him and his army. This introduces the theme of returning to the LORD in mourning (v. 12), with special attention to the nature of God, who is compassionate and caring. Thus the nation can expect Yahweh's blessing.

Sounding the Alarm (2:1-2a)

The *shophar* (RSV "trumpet"), or ram's horn, was used for sounding signals in a wide range of situations, including war (Ezek.

33:2-4), lamentation, and on ritual occasions such as the beginning of the Sabbath. Joel calls the priests to sound the alarm "in Zion" the holy city, summoning the people to prepare against the coming crisis. Similar calls are to be found in Jer. 4:5; 6:1; 51:27; Hos. 5:8; and elsewhere, but in Joel the reason for the call is that the "day of the LORD" approaches. "Gloom" and "darkness" are terms which have various applications. They may denote God's presence (cf. Deut. 4:11; Zeph. 1:15), but they may also describe the terror of God's absence (cf. Exod. 10:21; Ps. 107:10-14; Job 10:21-22; etc.). Here Joel applies them to the enemy's approach (cf. v. 10). Joel thus says that "the day," in which Yahweh comes to make himself and his will known, approaches along with the enemy troops. Although the enemy invasion which led to the present crisis was a thing of the past, Joel speaks of it as a current event to make more vivid his presentation.

The Enemy Advances (2:2b-10)

A special feature of this subsection is its use of seven metaphors describing the advancing army. Both the coming "day" and the advancing army are likened to darkness spreading across the mountains about Jerusalem. "Great" (Heb. *rab,* meaning vast numbers) and "powerful" (*'atsum*) refer to the invaders and are key words in this subsection (cf. vv. 5, 11). To emphasize the extent of the danger, Joel draws on the expression used in 1:2-3 that this event is unlike any previous one and will never be repeated.

In v. 3 Joel again uses the fire metaphor to describe the "scorched earth" policy of the enemy. The "before and after" theme is a leading feature that Joel now introduces and will use throughout vv. 3-15. The bounty of the land that was Eden-like has disappeared as the all-consuming troops sweep forward, leaving only devastation behind them (cf. ch. 1). By this metaphor Joel reverses the expression in Isa. 51:3 and Ezek. 36:35.

As the metaphors continue, we note in vv. 4-5 a reference both to the consuming fire and to the speed with which the enemy advances. The picture is of mounted troops speeding in chariots from mountaintop to mountaintop, barely touching the ground as it were. There is an interesting wordplay in this verse, as the word "war horse" (*parash*) in v. 4 is similar to the verb "scatter" (*parus*) in v. 2.

In vv. 6-9 Joel pictures the terror on the faces of those confronting the invading army. "Before it" (RSV "them") in v. 6 links with the "before and after" theme central to our passage, and implies that shortly the people will cease to exist, having been consumed by the enemy. The relentless and disciplined march of the enemy troops is such that no defense is effective. In this picture, Joel recalls the locust imagery of ch. 1. This description of the enemy advance is bound together by the use of common vocabulary ("run," "climb," and "wall") in vv. 7 and 9.

In a second picture (v. 10) of what has happened ahead of this army, Joel turns to yet another image. The whole universe, he says, "sun," "moon," and "stars," has panicked before it. The language is similar to that used in v. 2, but more important is the close relationship of 2:1-11 to Isa. 13, where so many of Joel's images apparently originate. Although Joel has drawn upon ideas in Isa. 13, his distinctive "before and after" theme is the framework into which those ideas have been set. Again we note the link in Joel's mind between the enemy advance and the "day of the LORD," as he speaks of both in terms of cosmic upheaval.

Turn to Yahweh (2:11-14)

A fourth application of the "before and after" theme occurs in this subsection in which it is Yahweh who acts and speaks. Joel envisages Yahweh as the general in command of his troops. Like the invading enemy army, Yahweh's army is both "numerous" (RSV "exceedingly great") and "powerful" (cf. v. 2). The careful use of these two adjectives allows Joel to make a pointed contrast between the two forces doing battle. The question which this verse raises for us is the meaning of the term "his [Yahweh's] host." It appears at first sight as though this is a reference to the enemy, a host or army which Yahweh has raised, in which case its function will be to bring judgment upon Judah. We have already noted that Joel nowhere mentions Judah's sin, so that we must doubt that Yahweh's troops are actually the enemy which Judah now faces. Furthermore, the function of the "before and after" theme is to contrast what the enemy troops leave behind them — disaster — and what Yahweh leaves behind — his blessing. For these reasons it would seem best to interpret "his army" as a general reference to the heavenly hosts which are at Yahweh's disposal. These are more powerful and numerous (RSV "exceedingly great," Heb. *rab me'od*) than the advancing enemy. This affirmation about Yahweh's troops then forms the basis of the call in vv. 12-14 for Judah to trust Yahweh for victory.

In a series of three clauses each beginning with "for," we see Yahweh (v. 11) as the leader of a vast army. The phrase "he . . . executes his word" is a parallel reference to the agent who responds to the divine call. This must relate to the LORD's "army" which attends to his voice (v. 11a). The third "for" clause is the climactic one, speaking of the "day of the LORD" as so fearful that nobody can endure it. In this way Joel anticipates a decisive confrontation between the ever-advancing army and the more powerful troops of Yahweh. That imminent conflict will mark the "day of the LORD," a day of Yahweh's victory in which he will restore what Judah's enemies destroyed. This theme is related closely to that of Yahweh as judge in 3:1-4, 9-18.

In view of Yahweh's power and the imminent conflict, Joel speaks for Yahweh (v. 12) and calls upon Judah to turn immediately and wholeheartedly to him. The mourning rites, which include fasting, weeping, and wearing of special clothing, express Judah's absolute dependence on divine aid.

What does Joel mean when he says (v. 13) "Rend your hearts and not your garments"? Does he really mean to discourage them from tearing their clothes as the lament ritual requires? He seems to mean that as well as tearing their clothing, an outward sign of lament, they also and more importantly need to show heartfelt lament about the current crisis. By using this form of speech Joel calls for a deep inner response in the lament. To suggest that he calls for an act of repentance can only be valid if the purpose of the lamenting is penitential. Lacking any other supporting evidence in the book or in the lament literature generally, we must conclude that penitence is not what Joel has in mind here. He intends to call the nation to a wholehearted response in pleading for God's assistance in their present difficulty. Joel's meaning and the Church's liturgical use of the verse with penitential emphasis differ markedly.

Those who participate in the lament ritual indicate that they have nowhere to turn but to God, and that their hope rests only in the character of God, in his graciousness, mercy, patience, and love (cf. Exod. 34:6, 7 and similar descriptions of God in Ps. 86:15; 103:8; 145:8; Neh. 9:17; Jonah 3:9; 4:2). In many human situations marked by gross injustice, oppression, or calamity, we may feel as Joel did, that there is no other way than to depend utterly upon God for deliverance. This is not to say that there may not be some human instrumentality through which God may bring about that deliverance. However, Joel's emphasis is entirely on God as Savior, as the one who brings life out of death.

The hope that God might "repent of evil" does not mean that God has done something wrong of which he must now repent. The verb *naham* can also mean to change one's plan (Gen. 6:6).

The word "evil" *(ra°)* often means something terrifying or frightful, rather than an immoral act (cf. Amos 7:3, 6; Jonah 3:10).

If Judah turns to him, Yahweh will turn to them. Such mutual action is, in v. 14, expressed in a rhetorical question, "Who knows whether . . . ?" (cf. v. 11). This is a way of emphasizing that Yahweh's aid is absolutely certain. Another way of putting it is to say, "We know that Yahweh will turn and bless us." When Yahweh marches before his people he leaves behind blessing (v. 14a), or, to reuse the image from 1:10, he provides the community with grain and wine. The grain and wine in turn will be used to express joy and thankfulness to God. In vv. 13-14 there are two echoes from the book of Jonah—Jonah 4:2 in Joel 2:13; Jonah 3:9 in Joel 2:14a. These have also been incorporated into Joel's "before and after" theme, although the final subsection turns that theme around significantly—the enemy troops left behind destruction, but Yahweh leaves behind blessing. This reversal of the theme at its climax introduces the note of hope and consolation to follow. The longing expressed in the lament sets the tone for the next stage of the lament ritual, but first Joel records another Cry of Alarm.

CRY OF ALARM, II (2:15-17)

Just as we noted that Joel records two Cries of Lament (1:15-18, 19-20), so too do we find two Cries of Alarm. This second and briefer Cry uses the same opening phrase as 2:1, and it continues as does the first Cry with a series of imperative and jussive verbal forms which together urge the people of Judah to gather to plead for God's help.

The Cry uses terms found already in 1:14, a fact which associates this Cry of Alarm with the Call to Lamentation in 1:13-14. Here in 2:15-16, however, we also detect a duplicated structure, the first part of which is in 2:15bc-16a, and the second part in 2:16bcd. Both parts commence with a call to sanctification and end with a summons to gather together; the first part urges a response in lament rites, the second specifies who it is who should respond—in this case, the entire nation, young and old alike. This Cry of Alarm, which appeals to Judah to prepare for battle, is extended in v. 16e to incorporate bride and bridegroom, that is, those normally exempt from military service (cf. Deut. 20:7; 24:5). To emphasize the seriousness of the moment, Joel sets a precedent, for never before have infants, children, old people, and honeymooning couples been called up for military duty. This matches what Joel says in 1:2-3 about the unprecedented nature of the crisis.

In 2:17 we meet again a reference to "priests" and "ministers" (cf. 1:9, 13). Their cry of lament is to include a call for deliverance, that Yahweh might take pity on his people in their plight. The altar referred to stands before the temple, so we picture the priests praying between the altar of burnt offerings and the entrance to the temple building proper. Judah, God's own people, his "possession" (Exod. 19:5), faced the shame of falling into enemy hands. The fear that Judah will become a "reproach," or be shamed, is an expression met with in lament psalms (cf. Ps. 22:7; 69:10, 11, 20; 71:13; 74:22; 79:12; etc.), and has to do with being ruled over by foreigners. It also relates to the damage done to God's "reputation," because Judah's enemies have depended upon the assistance of their own gods in overthrowing Judah. In defeat it appears that Yahweh is powerless to aid his people, and so together they are scorned. The idea that Yahweh on occasion acts in order to "save face" is understandable in an Eastern context. It is a very human way of speaking about God, but it is highly expressive (cf. Num. 14:13-19; 1 Sam. 17:26; Ezek. 36:15). The concluding quotation of the enemy's taunt is identical to that in Ps. 79:10 (cf. also 42:10), and reflects the fear expressed frequently in the lament psalms that God has abandoned his people (cf. Ps. 3:2; 10:1-4; 22:1; etc.); otherwise why would such a critical situation have arisen?

Thus far in Joel we have noted a collection of various literary units and forms, such as the Summons, the Call to Lamentation, the Cry of Lament, and the Cry of Alarm, all clearly related to a lament setting. From this we may affirm that behind the book in its present form there lies a lament liturgy, elements of which Joel preserves. The fact that some elements, such as the Cry of Lament and the Cry of Alarm, occur twice suggests that the lament liturgy was used on more than one occasion. From the prophet's responses which we shall meet in ch. 3, we conclude that there were at least four occasions upon which Joel presided, in a prophetic-priestly role, at this kind of ritual.

YAHWEH'S RESPONSE (2:18-27)

A turning point comes in the book of Joel at 2:18. In 1:1 – 2:17 Joel spoke of an impending disaster and called the people of Judah to face it prayerfully. Beginning in 2:18 we find a collection of statements oriented toward the future and all promising Judah

a brighter hope for tomorrow. There is a change in the direction
and purpose of Joel's message; he now addresses the response to
the people's lament. In 2:18-27, 28-32 we read of Yahweh's response to the plea uttered in lamentation, while in ch. 3 four
other responses are found, all of which come from the prophet
himself. A common feature of each of these responses is that
Judah is assured that the enemy will be dealt with appropriately.
In order to highlight the message of this portion of the book, we
follow the structure Joel has provided and divide 2:18-27 into
four subsections as follows: 2:18, 19-20, 21-23, 24-27.

In 2:18 we meet Joel's editorial comment which links the Cry
of Alarm II (2:15-17) with Yahweh's response to that cry in vv.
19-20—note the key word "reproach" in both v. 17 and v. 19.
Yahweh's reply to Judah's plea for help is described as arising
from a "jealousy" *(qana')* for her. Here the word "jealous" differs
from its modern sense; it describes God's zeal for and devotion
to his people and land. It is obvious from v. 18 that the lament
ritual moved Yahweh to do something for his suffering people as
well as to "save face," so we are correct in assuming that the
lament ritual has moved on to the next stage and that Judah
awaits the result of their petition for divine help. As to how God
responded, we need to read on.

19-20   Yahweh speaks directly to his people's plea for help by
echoing the metaphor of food shortage used in 1:10. God himself
will replenish the stores of "grain, wine, and oil" (v. 19b) destroyed by the enemy troops, presumably by assuring a good
harvest the following season. Also, in contrast to their present
shortage of food, Yahweh undertakes to supply enough to satisfy
all their needs. They will have adequate food both to eat and to
use for sacrifice. A second statement (v. 19c) promises that Judah
will no more be shamed by other nations. Neither they nor Yahweh
will become the object of scorn by others again. It is by delivering
his people from their current crisis that Yahweh will recover his
reputation as one who is able to save, as one who has not abandoned his people. The faithfulness of God stands as the founda-
tion of his people's trust in him.

In further confirmation of his aid, Yahweh promises to reverse
the present calamitous situation (v. 20). How will he do so? He
will send the oppressor—the "northerner" is a traditional term
for Judah's enemy (see Jer. 1:14-15; 6:1; Ezek. 38:6; 39:2)—far off
into a barren desert, a place of devastation similar to that which
they have brought upon Judah. Their leading troops, says Joel,

will be sent into the "eastern" or Dead Sea, and the rearguard will be driven west to the Mediterranean. In addition, the "stench" of their dead troops will offend and be a further embarrassment to the enemy (cf. Isa. 34:3; Amos 4:10). The nations and their gods will thus lose face.

The concluding phrase in v. 20 explains why Yahweh will help Judah directly by providing food, as well as indirectly by scattering the enemy. The reason given for Yahweh's actions is that the enemy has, in its pride, sought greatness for itself. This then represents the reverse side of the enemy's defiant challenge to Judah— "Where is your God?" Their haughty attitude expresses one motive for their attack on Judah, namely, that it was for their own glory that they invaded Judah and defiled Yahweh's sanctuary. Yahweh must respond to such a challenge.

21-23 From first-person speech by Yahweh in 2:19-20 we move to third-person speech about him. The section 2:21-23 is significant for several reasons: the presence of imperative forms, which dominate these verses; the call to put aside fear and celebrate God's impending victory; the further application of the "reversal" principle as Yahweh proclaims the onset of rain to end the drought and provide a bountiful harvest.

The theme of this brief section is summarized in v. 21; Joel calls on the land to shed its fear and to rejoice. The reason for this is clear—Yahweh has exalted himself. The latter is in deliberate contrast to the self-exaltation of the nations in v. 20. As Joel expands the thought of v. 21, he repeats the call to cast off fear (v. 22) and addresses it to the beasts of the field. The Almighty exalts himself for their sakes by providing fodder, and so the ravages of "drought" and "fire" (1:19-20) are to be undone. The "fig tree" and "vine" will no longer refuse to yield their "fruit" (contra 1:7). By using verbal forms which indicate that the action is completed, Joel is saying that as Yahweh has promised to restore the land's fertility, it is as good as accomplished already.

The second imperative of v. 21 ("be glad!") is elaborated in v. 23. Joel invites the inhabitants of Jerusalem to turn from lament to celebration. What a change will come about as Yahweh sends rain to quench the flame and end the drought! Both images, flame and drought, are derived from ch. 1. Although restoration of the land's bounty is an impending event, Joel again speaks of it as already accomplished by using a perfect verb form, *natan* ("has given").

One phrase in v. 23 has been a constant problem for interpreters. The phrase *litsedaqah* may be rendered as "for right," "for vindication." Is this then a reference to Yahweh's righteousness? In Wolff's view (*Joel*, 63), the rain and subsequent harvest are expressions of the covenant relationship which Yahweh has with Judah. However, the feminine form *tsedaqah*, as in Isa. 45:8 and Hos. 10:12, refers to that which springs up from the ground. In Prov. 8:18 it indicates "prosperity." This sense seems appropriate in the present context. Because Yahweh is Judah's God, he will send the rain, in this way reversing the "drought" and providing the people with crops. This provision will be the nation's "prosperity," its *tsedaqah*.

We have already set forward grounds for believing that lamentation in Joel is unrelated to the idea of repentance, for none is required. In addition, if we consider the date and circumstances of the book, we conclude that the situation being lamented was the destruction caused by the invading Babylonian armies some fifty years earlier, a destruction still visible in Jerusalem. From this vantage point we may affirm, with Deutero-Isaiah (40:2), that Judah's punishment was indeed over, she had long since paid for her sins. Now, with that behind her, the return of the land's bounty would express in a concrete way Judah's new "prosperity."

24-27 With v. 24 we return again to first-person speech as Yahweh confirms his plan to restore all that was destroyed by the invading armies. Numerous terms here recall the opening words of Yahweh's response in 2:19 — "grain," "wine," "oil," "satisfy," "send," "never again be ashamed" — and so provide the connecting ideas throughout the section 2:18-27.

In vv. 24-25 Yahweh promises that food produced in Judah will again be available in abundance; once more the traditional terms "grain," "wine," and "oil" describe the bounty. "Threshing floors," level hard-surfaced places for separating the grain from the husks, are similar to areas used throughout Asia for drying the rice following the harvest. These, and the storage vats for the juice from newly trodden grapes, will not be large enough to hold all that God provides. God's plan is to restore or complete *(shalam)* what had been lost to the "locusts" (1:4).

The expression *heli haggadol* (v. 25) is translated as "my great army." Our task is to determine its meaning. Bearing in mind Joel's context, we conclude that the "locusts" or the "great army," which here are in parallel, refer back to the original Babylonian invasion. That enemy incursion was, according to the earlier prophetic witness, God's doing, for it came as a means of divine judgment. But the devastation which the enemy brought will now be reversed (cf. 2:1-14); Yahweh will restore what "his great army" demolished. In this way Joel assures and comforts the lamenting returnees with the promise that the land will return to its former happier state.

The connection which v. 26 has to the thought of v. 19 is also apparent. Two themes are repeated: the first, the satisfaction which God gives; the second, the reversal of Judah's embarrassment before its enemies. Rather than the "locusts" and "fire" eating their crops, Judah itself will now eat and be sated, with the result that Yahweh will be praised (cf. v. 23). In addition, the reversal of the present crisis will bring permanent honor for Judah (vv. 26, 27) and thus indirectly for Yahweh. All of this discounts the enemy's scoffing (v. 17) and can be traced back to Yahweh's reaction spoken of in v. 18, that Yahweh was "jealous for his land" and "had pity on his people."

In v. 27 Joel raises an important theological issue, namely, the *purpose* of God's action on Judah's behalf. Joel affirms that God's actions are the means whereby he makes himself known (cf. also 3:17). Deutero-Isaiah is the foremost spokesman for this formulation (see Isa. 45:5-6, 22; 46:9; etc.), and Ezekiel sounds a similar theme (Ezek. 13:14, 21, 23, etc.). We note three elements in Joel's presentation: he suggests that what Yahweh will do is for the purpose of letting Judah know (1) that Yahweh is in its midst— he has not, as the nations have suggested (2:17), abandoned his people. This same concern is expressed in many of the lament psalms (cf., e.g., Ps. 22:1). God is *with* his people in their sufferings. Indeed, on the basis of Rom. 5:6-8 we can go further and claim that God in Christ suffers *for* us; (2) that Yahweh is Judah's God—thus that their relationship as parties to a covenant continues. This implies that their present anguish is not to be taken as evidence of a broken relationship, a view inconsistent with the Davidic covenant as an "everlasting" covenant; and (3) that there is no other God than Yahweh. For this reason Judah need not fear other so-called gods and those who serve them. The powers of this world are ultimately impotent before God (cf. Rom. 8:31-39); his actions on our behalf are the living proof of that.

The monotheism which Joel expresses—that there is no deity other than Yahweh—is something we know already from Deutero-Isaiah. In Israel's earlier history, for example, in the first of the Ten Commandments (Exod. 20:2-3), we meet the view that as far as Israel is concerned there is only one deserving of their worship, that is, Yahweh. Other gods may exist, but Israel must have nothing to do with them. By the time the Exile in Babylon is concluding, however, that view has altered to the point that Israel denies the existence of all other deities.

PROPHETIC PROMISES (2:28-32)

A little-used prophetic introduction (see Isa. 1:26; Jer. 16:16; 21:7) marks this section off from Yahweh's response. We note, however, a close relationship with the overall lament setting.

28-29 The first two verses are bound together by a common phrase: "I will pour out my spirit." God's "spirit" or "breath" *(ruah)* is that energizing power given for use in his service (cf. Exod. 35:31; Judg. 3:10; etc.). Two features are important to the giving of God's spirit as mentioned here: (1) The timing. The gift of the Spirit will follow some other, apparently unspecified, event. We presume it relates to the period when the current crisis is reversed. That is, the Spirit will be given during the restoration already promised (2:18-27). Part of that restoration will include the energetic presence of God within the entire community. Just as the Alarm Cry went out to all, young and old alike, to join in the lamentation (2:16), so now God will bestow on all his divine presence. (2) The nature of the event. According to Joel it will include "all flesh" *(kol-basar)*. Though this term could include all living creatures, it most likely refers to every member of the restored community of Judah. Furthermore, the Spirit's presence will manifest itself in prophecy, dreams, and visions, which traditionally are ways in which God communicates with his people. Thus God has not abandoned them, despite the outward appearance of devastation. In a short time, Judah will know once more, says Joel, the physical reminders of God's presence with them.

The background for the thought in 2:28-29 would appear to be Ezek. 39:25-29, an oracle in which Ezekiel promises restoration from among the nations, no more shame for Judah, together with the additional promise that Judah will know Yahweh their God. The last two promises Joel has already conveyed to Judah (2:19, 26-27). The promise of vv. 28-29 is linked to that of v. 27 and is the tangible evidence of God's abiding presence. The total context of restoration from among the nations and the pouring out of God's Spirit not only links with earlier promises but also provides the introduction to the oracles against foreign nations that follow.

In Acts 2:16-18, Peter at Pentecost quotes Joel 2:28-29, giving the impression that what Joel had in mind was specifically the Pentecost event. We can see that Joel himself spoke to his contemporaries who were in need of comfort during a national crisis. Further, his vision was restricted to an event in Judah. He does not envisage this event embracing Gentiles; Peter does (Acts 2:39). From several points of view it is clear that Joel's original intention and what the early Church understood it to be are not identical. Therefore, to say that the latter "fulfils" the former, in the sense that it is the direct result of a word spoken earlier by Joel, is inappropriate. On the other hand, that Peter quoted this text to interpret an event in his own day is highly significant. Peter publicly proclaims thereby that the God who was active in Joel's day was similarly active in his own time, that the emerging Christian community has a direct association with the past. It is a claim that in Jesus we meet with God's new method of communicating with humanity, that in Jesus God's energetic presence, his "spirit," has been witnessed afresh. Even more significant is that God's new act went far beyond that in Joel's time, for the gospel embraced all peoples. What Joel saw as God's gift to a needy Judah, Peter claimed for all humanity.

30-32 Here we note a different subject matter — cosmic signs or "portents" which precede "the day of Yahweh" and which point to its approach. The terms "blood," "fire," "smoke," and "darkness" are frequently, though not exclusively, associated with the divine presence and speak of God's might and majesty. "Fire" and "darkness" are also terms which Joel has used to depict the enemy invasion which led to the present crisis (cf. 1:19-20; 2:2, 3, 5, 10). "Blood" and "smoke," though not previously mentioned, are also descriptive of the battle. In 2:11 Joel has already spoken of the fearfulness of "the day of Yahweh"; he now reiterates it. However, here we detect a new significance, one consistent with the theme of restoration. The present crisis, a prelude to "the day of Yahweh" (2:11), actually anticipates the day of restoration. We should note that in these words of consolation and promise, "the day" is viewed as a day of salvation for God's people, not one of judgment. The "terror" of that day is that of God's presence himself.

Joel gives Judah another vantage point from which to view the calamity that has struck them, by suggesting that the actual destruction which they see about them is a sign of hope. On the one hand, as we shall see in ch. 3, the present devastation indicates what the future will be for the nations who have caused such hardship for Judah. On the other hand, Joel argues that the sights and sounds of battle themselves may be seen as signs of coming peace, brought by Yahweh's own presence. Only the eye of faith could interpret the current devastation in those terms. Joel quotes from another prophetic response to a national lament, citing Obad. 17-18, to underscore God's salvation. The reference is to Zion and Jerusalem because that city is the focus for the promises Yahweh has made to Judah through the house of David. In this way Joel reminds the sorry inhabitants of Judah that despite the present dismal situation, Yahweh's eternal covenant with them will bear fruit. Those who call on Yahweh are those whom he will call (cf. Hos. 11:1) and name as his own.

In Rom. 10:13 Paul refers to the promise of Joel 2:32 that "every one who calls upon the name of the Lord will be saved." There is an obvious disparity between Joel's original message of comfort to his contemporaries and the meaning given it by Paul, who contends that salvation includes both Jews and Greeks. However, it is just that difference which helps us clarify the early Church's attitude to the OT Scriptures, namely, that free quotation was an accepted method for establishing the continuity of faith represented by the early Church. Paul's expansion of Joel's words represents a bold assertion that the wide embrace of the gospel of Christ and his Church stood firmly in the old faith tradition. In addition, the early Church, by using a method of interpretation familiar to the rabbis and other Jewish groups, claimed for the church at least an equality with the synagogue as inheritors of the true faith. Such a claim has important consequences in today's Jewish-Christian dialogue.

One other difference between these two passages calls for comment. Joel's idea of "deliverance" is principally that of a reversal of the current national crisis — the land will again flourish with crops, and Judah will not be shamed by other nations. It is a visible and tangible change in Judah's welfare that Joel announces. As for Paul's use of the term in Rom. 10:13, we see immediately that "salvation" has another connotation. It certainly is not national restoration; rather, it is the opportunity, across every national barrier, for people to enter into fellowship with God. Such a new relationship will affect personal and national welfare, but it also has wider implications which include the continuance of that fellowship beyond death.

CHAPTER 3

GOD'S JUDGMENT ON
JUDAH'S ENEMIES

FOUR ORACLES AGAINST FOREIGN NATIONS (3:1-21)

This chapter records four oracles each directed against Israel's enemies. Beginning at least from the 8th cent. B.C., other prophets also used this form of address (cf. Isa. 13–19; Jer. 46–51; Ezek. 27–28; etc.). When we understand that Israel's prophets spoke essentially to their own generation and countrymen, we may ask what purpose they had in speaking to them about foreign nations and the divine judgment that would come upon them. Clearly this news is not primarily for the nations to hear, but for Israel. We may detect different purposes, particularly relating to preparations for war and to lamentation (see J. H. Hayes, "The Usage of Oracles against Foreign Nations in Ancient Israel," *JBL* 87 [1968] 87). In view of the lament setting of this book, we understand these oracles as the prophet's responses to national laments.

Each oracle serves to comfort Judah, assuring it that God will judge the enemy which caused the present crisis. In the case of Joel, these oracles complement Yahweh's response (2:18-27) and the promises found in 2:28-32. In 2:18-27, 28-32 we have noted direct associations between those responses and the Call to Lamentation and Cries of Alarm in 1:4–2:17. This would imply that the officiating prophet referred back to elements in the liturgy in framing an appropriate response to that lament. In addition to this reference back to elements in the liturgy used, we are able to detect in 3:1-21 connections with other lament psalms. This is similar to the situation with Obadiah and Jer. 49:7-22, both of which are directly related to Ps. 137. The fact that Joel on several occasions in ch. 3 quotes from Obadiah adds to our information about prophetic oracles against foreign nations and their function as responses to national laments.

Each of the foreign nation oracles (3:1-3, 4-8, 9-18, 19-21) is independent. The first and third oracles are general and the second and fourth are specific about the nation(s) concerned. It is from these responses that we learn of the historical circumstances in which the lament ritual behind the book of Joel was used, for here the prophet relates the words of comfort to the specific needs of the lamenters.

Oracle against the Nations, I (3:1-3)

The first foreign nation oracle begins with a composite phrase, used occasionally by Jeremiah (cf. 33:15; 50:4, 20), and continues with the verb "return" (RSV "restore," Heb. *shub*), a verb also typical of Jeremiah. The future to which the phrase refers is the time when Yahweh will reverse *('ashib)* Judah's crisis so that a similar crisis befalls the nations (cf. Isa. 43:3). Yahweh plans to *restore the fortunes* of Judah (cf. Jer. 15:19; 30:3; 31:23; Hos. 6:11; Amos 9:14), which means that God will give back what Judah had lost. This theme of reversal is one already used by Joel in 2:18-27. It is found in all four of the foreign nation oracles, albeit under different terms (cf. vv. 7-8, 18, 19). In Obadiah the verb *shub* is similarly used. Although we can document the prophetic usages of this theme, we should especially note its link with the plea found in a number of laments (e.g., Ps. 28:4 and 53:6).

In v. 2 the "valley of Jehoshaphat" is to be the scene of Yahweh's judgment of the nations (see also 3:12). The name "Jehoshaphat" is composed of two elements; "Jeho," which is an abbreviation of the Hebrew word we translate as "LORD," and the verb *shaphat*, which means "judge." The "valley of Jehoshaphat" is an expression found only in the book of Joel, and since such a location is impossible to identify, we assume that the name refers in a representative way to that place at which Yahweh will assemble peoples for judgment.

Two words are used to describe Judah — "my people" and "my heritage." The first of these has been used in 2:18, 27 and has a broad background in the covenant tradition. It is that covenant relationship which prompts Yahweh to respond to Judah's plea (2:18). The second term refers to the land given Judah by God, and, by extension, to those who occupy it. We note in lament psalms (Ps. 28:9; 74:2; 79:1; etc.) that both terms are used to identify Israel.

The nature of the offense with which the nations are charged is the rape of Judah. This is described by a series of five actions — *scatter, divide, cast lots for, give, sell* — all of which echo the complaint sections of national laments (cf. Ps. 22:18; 44:11-12; Lam. 5:2) and other oracles against foreign nations (Obad. 11; Jer. 50:17).

Apart from exiling Judah from its divinely given land and confiscating it, defenseless boys and girls were used as items for trade to satisfy the enemy's self-indulgence. Here, "boys" and "girls" are used together as a parallel expression to "my people."

If this brief oracle is Joel's response to a specific lament ritual, our next question is whether we can determine that historical situation. The community devastated and exiled is Judah and Jerusalem (v. 1), so the most likely crisis is the Babylonian incursions of 597 B.C. and 587 B.C. The several connections with Jeremiah noted in this response strengthen that possibility. Thus it seems highly likely that Joel 3:1-3 preserves the prophet's message of comfort in a lament ritual following Jerusalem's destruction by Babylon. The text of v. 2 states clearly that it is "all the nations" who will come to judgment. We presume this means all who participated with Babylon in the attack on Jerusalem. As to how much later than the actual event the ritual was held, we consider two factors: (1) Joel borrowed from Obadiah; thus we place the lament some time after the return to Jerusalem in 538 B.C., but prior to the successful restoration of the new community. (2) As Obadiah and Jer. 49 testify, lament over the destruction of Jerusalem continued well beyond the devastation itself, through the time in exile, and on into the early days of the restoration. This means that the pain of that event was still felt keenly for more than sixty years; no doubt the anguish revived at the sight of the still devastated city and temple in 538, the year in which the Persian king Cyrus permitted the exiles of Judah to return to Jerusalem. Joel assures Judah that all nations who were party to the rape of the land would suffer the same fate themselves. Even though at that point it may have seemed as though justice was rather late in coming, yet the prophet insists that justice will be done.

Oracle against the Nations, II (3:4-8)

The second foreign nation oracle is unlike the first since it has no introductory clause, although it does have a prophetic-type conclusion (cf. Obad. 18). It addresses a coastal confederation, Tyre and Sidon along with Philistia. The same group is addressed by Jeremiah in 47:4 in the context of an oracle against the Philistines. Tyre and Sidon are cities on the Phoenician coast. "Philistia" describes a more southerly group of five cities on Israel's coastal plain. Apparently these powers acted together against Judah (cf. Ps. 83:7; Ezek. 16:57), hence Joel pronounces God's judgment against them.

The oracle opens with two rhetorical questions (v. 4). The first is a forceful statement that the confederation is insignificant in God's sight. The second ironically asks whether these foreigners intend to "pay" God "back" for something he did to them. Yahweh responds by pointing out that any such action would be swiftly repaid. Both questions express God's contempt for the confederacy's actions. What did these nations do? The first accusation against them (v. 5) is that they plundered Jerusalem, carrying off its treasures as spoil. A second charge (v. 6) is that they sold *(makar)* Judahites to foreigners (cf. also v. 8ab; Amos 1:6, 9; Ezek. 27:13), as did the nations mentioned in 3:1-3.

The main verb in 3:4-8 is "pay back" *(gamal)*. We should note carefully its use, as it occurs four times, three of them in v. 4. The confederation is charged with trying to "repay" God for something, but Yahweh will have the final word and "pay back" their evil. Joel points to these evil deeds as actual signs of God's salvation (cf. 2:18-27). The retribution principle in these foreign nation oracles is carried by this verb *gamal*. We find the verb in the cry for deliverance in several lament psalms (cf. Ps. 28:4; 94:2; 137:7), and it is a key term in the responsive words of assurance in other foreign nation oracles (cf. Obad. 15). That Joel uses the concept in a manner similar to Obadiah we conclude from his quotation of Obad. 15 in vv. 4, 7: "I will requite your deed on your own head" (cf. P. Miller, *Sin and Judgment*, pp. 75-76, 97-110).

Selling Judahites to the distant Greeks is both the reason for, and the manner in which, God will pay back the confederacy. The enemy will be sold to another power, the Sabeans, a people far to the south of Judah (Jer. 6:20; 1 Kgs. 10:2). The operative word in these balanced actions is "far off"; the nations sent Judah far from its own home in one direction, so God will send Judah's enemies as far away in the other direction.

Another key word in this oracle is "stir up" *('ur)*, a little-used verb found three times in this chapter, as well as in several lament psalms (Ps. 7:6; 35:23; 44:23; etc.). In these psalms the petitioner calls on Yahweh to bestir himself and act on behalf of his people. In Joel 3:7 the prophet assures Judah that Yahweh will "stir up" his exiled people. Thus, in addition to punishing the enemies, God's "stirring" signals Judah's own restoration.

We note that Yahweh is the primary actor in this drama. He is lord of history, of *all* history, and on this basis Joel can assure Judah that the present crisis is in God's hands. Yahweh's aid to Judah in this oracle depends not primarily on the special relationship or covenant between himself and the people of Judah, but rather on the fact that plunder and disregard for persons is an offense against Yahweh himself. We note a similar line of argument in Amos 1 – 2. Even though during the monarchy there may have been some treaty relationship among the various groups Amos mentions, yet it would appear that the prophets contended that there was among all peoples a basic understanding of what ethical conduct is acceptable. Wherever this is disregarded, Yahweh may step in and bring judgment.

In Joel's view, the task of righting injustice lies not in the hands of fallible human beings and movements, but with a just God. Joel 2:12-14 called Judah to trust unswervingly in Yahweh as they faced their current dilemma. Similarly, in this oracle, Joel's basic premise is that Yahweh *alone* will correct injustice. Also, Yahweh's demand for justice is universal and not bound only to those who recognize some special relationship with him (see the Excursus below).

Can we determine when Joel spoke this oracle, or to what it refers historically? K. Elliger maintains that there is little concrete evidence of such a coastal confederation until the later Persian period, that is, during the mid-4th cent. B.C. (see "Ein Zeugnis aus der jüdischen Gemeinde im Alexanderjahr 332 v. Chr.," *ZAW* 62 [1950] 63-115). As several scholars (e.g., J. Bright, *Jeremiah,* 312) date Jer. 47:4 to the Babylonian period of ca. 605 B.C., however, we may maintain an early sixth-century date if necessary. References to Javan (Greece) and the Sabeans are not of significant historical value, for both appear primarily as references to distant locations. They are representative terms rather than actual trading partners, although we do know of trade between the Greeks and Tyre before 587 B.C. (see J. Myers, "Some Considerations Bearing on the Date of Joel," *ZAW* 74 [1962] 177-95). The charge that the confederation plundered Jerusalem and sold Judahites must predate the Exile, and the possibility is raised that these coastal neighbors assisted Babylon or at least took advantage of the situation, as did Edom, when Jerusalem was razed in 587 B.C. This is certainly what Ezek. 25:15 – 26:6 has in mind.

Oracle against the Nations, III (3:9-18)

The third and longest of the foreign nation oracles is a general oracle against the nations similar to 3:1-3 and bearing some of the same themes. It divides into two parts, as indicated by verbs in the imperative in vv. 9-13 and verbal forms in the imperfect that dominate vv. 14-18. This division indicates the two directions in which the oracle moves: the first is a summons to the nations to gather for judgment; the second is the assurance to Judah that Yahweh will be a refuge, that the present crisis will be turned into a new future.

As we listen to Joel we hear him in v. 9 employ two verbs, "call" (RSV "proclaim") and "sanctify" (RSV "prepare"), used earlier in the summons to lament (1:14; 2:15), and a third verb "stir up," which he has used in the preceding oracle (3:7). On this occasion these verbs are all directed to Judah's enemies, as Yahweh calls upon the foreign troops to prepare to confront divine justice (cf. Obad. 1). In other circumstances, such as Jer. 6:4, the call to battle is part of the call to embark upon a holy war, a passionate crusade for Yahweh, but here Joel employs them to call the nations to prepare to meet Yahweh.

A feature of Joel's writing observed already is his use of quotations, in particular quotations from other prophets. In v. 10 Joel skilfully reverses a text from Isa. 2:4 (cf. Mic. 4:3) and calls the nations to ready themselves for battle by crafting weapons from their farming implements. Even the weakest member is urged to think of himself as a warrior and to participate in the confrontation with Yahweh.

Further imperatives in v. 11 add a sense of urgency to the prophet's call for the nations to assemble. The final phrase of v. 11, "Bring down thy warriors, O LORD," has caused some difficulties for interpreters, and the ancient texts have various suggestions as to its meaning. Two factors seem important to bear in mind in any attempt to solve this question: (1) the direction of the imperatives in vv. 9-12 is toward the nations and the LORD is the speaker; (2) the use of the verb "shatter" (*hatat*, Hiphil) in two other foreign nation oracles, Obad. 9 and Jer. 49:37, which speak of what Yahweh will do to the enemy. In view of these two factors, it is best to translate v. 11b not as the RSV does, calling on Yahweh to bring down his warriors, but as "Yahweh will shatter your warriors," a warning to the nations of what is to come. This alteration is consistent with other textual traditions, namely, the Targum Jonathan and the Vulgate, and has the added advantage of bringing v. 11 closer to the thought of v. 12b. In v. 12 Yahweh reiterates the call of v. 9 that the nations arouse themselves, then demands they come up to Jehoshaphat, the place of Yahweh's judgment (cf. v. 2). The second half of v. 12 introduces a purpose clause using "for" *(ki)*. This is significant, for it denotes the reason for issuing all the preceding imperatives in vv

9-12. Yahweh sits enthroned as universal judge, a role already mentioned in 3:2.

Verse 13 demonstrates Joel's literary skill as he heaps up three brief imperatives with attached purpose clauses. His skill is especially evident in the way he combines (1) the theme of the reversal of disaster, which he has described as crop failure in ch. 1, and the subsequent bounty which Yahweh will provide (ch. 2); and (2) the theme of judgment of the nations. Reaping the harvest and treading the grapes speak of supplying Judah's needs for food, but they are at the same time expressions of judgment against the nations (cf. Mic. 4:13). We note Joel's irony in suggesting that their own farming implement, the "sickle," be the "weapon" of judgment.

The one addressed in v. 13 is not clearly identifiable. The call by Yahweh to execute the sentence passed on the nations is a general one, which does not specify who is to act. However, the call functions as a pivotal verse, for, judgment having been passed on the nations, the message of comfort turns toward Judah (vv. 14-18). In the closing phrase of v. 13 there is a single reference to the nations' wickedness. This is the cause of judgment against them. Details are not given except to note that their evil is great.

As Joel turns to express divine assurance for Judah's future (v. 14), he reuses ideas from the preceding Call to Lamentation and Cry of Alarm. The valley of Jehoshaphat is described as the valley of sentencing and judgment *(haruts)*, and it is crowded with people as the day of Yahweh's action approaches. The "crowd" imagery certainly relates to the hordes of enemy troops spoken of in ch. 1, and to the "locusts." The central theme, "the day of Yahweh," also comes from the earlier parts of the liturgy (1:15; 2:1, 11, 31). The "day" is that moment when Yahweh's judgment is meted out on the assembled enemies. To portray the awesomeness of that moment, Joel repeats the image of cosmic upheaval which spells darkness and gloom (cf. 2:3, 10, 31).

In the midst of this fearsome event stands Yahweh, Judah's refuge (v. 16). Several points are made here about Yahweh's person:

1. *Yahweh is a refuge to his people.* The vision of Yahweh roaring from Zion resembles Amos 1:2 and Hos. 11:10. It conveys two ideas: (a) the terror of Yahweh who appears as judge; (b) the lion fiercely protecting its offspring. Both aspects are of importance in this passage since the fearful judge is at the same time the protector of those in need. In several lament psalms (Ps. 31:2, 4; 43:2; 61:3) the petitioner pleads for Yahweh to provide exactly this kind of refuge against the enemy. Joel promises that in the

midst of crisis, God will be with his people and be their defense. On the one hand, he suffers with them, and on the other, he is their protector.

2. *Yahweh can be known in what he does for his people.* Joel insists that Yahweh's action in judging the nations and in protecting Judah will demonstrate his lordship, that thereby Judah will come to know God in a new way. In Ps. 83:13-18 we note a request that Yahweh make known his lordship by saving his people. Joel is able to concur in this idea — Yahweh's deeds express his being and person, thus making him known. Deutero-Isaiah most typifies this viewpoint, but we find it in Ezekiel also (e.g., 23:49; 24:27; 25:7, 11, 17), so we may assume that in late exilic times a special emphasis was being placed upon this interpretation of Yahweh's deeds.

3. *Yahweh dwells with his people and protects them.* In responding to the earlier lament, Joel repeats some of its ideas: for example, 2:27 has already spoken of Yahweh's acts and their significance for making him known. But there is probably a further significance in v. 17; it is to be viewed against the background of the taunt, "Where is their God?" (2:17), which the nations directed against Judah. To this specific challenge Joel responds with the assertion that God resides in Zion. From this affirmation we see once again the Davidic covenant tradition in which Joel stands. The presence of Yahweh is a sanctifying one (v. 17b). To describe Jerusalem as "holy" means that it is set aside for a special function, that is, it is the residence of the holy God. His holiness then makes the city and its inhabitants holy. In conjunction with this idea of holiness stands the notion that foreigners *(zarim)* are excluded from within its walls. In the context of assuring the anguished inhabitants of Jerusalem that God has heard their lament, Joel's meaning is obvious — Judah can be confident that enemy troops will not enter to plunder and rob again (cf. Obad. 11; Ezek. 7:21; 11:9).

4. *Yahweh will supply his people's needs.* Joel's assurance continues in v. 18 with a theme reminiscent of Yahweh's words in 2:24-26; both are pictures which reverse the situation described in 1:10-12, 17-18. Here, then, the "day of Yahweh" is seen from a perspective other than that of judgment — it is the time of God's blessing as drought and famine are ended. The bounty of the land will return; the mountains will drip with "juice" (RSV "sweet wine," Heb. *'asis;* cf. 1:5 and Amos 9:13 for other uses of this rare term) and "milk"; "streams" will "flow" again after the rains. This oracle climaxes in its vision of "the house of the LORD" as the

spring from which will gush waters to revive the thirsty land. We know of this imagery from Ezek. 47 and several Zion psalms (Ps. 46:4; 65:9), but Joel applies it as a description of God bringing to an end Judah's "drought" (cf. ch. 1).

Four times in ch. 1 Joel focuses the crisis facing Judah as occurring in the "house of the LORD" (1:9, 13, 14, 16), so appropriately his words of assurance relate the future blessing to that same "house." The valley of "Shittim" (acacia trees) is difficult to locate. Perhaps, like the valley of Jehoshaphat, it is not meant as a specific location.

Mention of actual place-names, such as Jerusalem and Zion, and the allusion to a "valley of Jehoshaphat" are understandable against the background of the Davidic covenant. Joel wants to apply his words of consolation to a specific people, the people of Judah, in a specific time and place. However, these place-names may for us be representative, meaning that God is not confined to working in those places, but will be known in judgment and in blessing wherever his people are at "home."

Some features in this third foreign nation oracle suggest a setting for this response. Connections with 3:1-3 — "the nation," "the valley of Jehoshaphat" — prompt us to associate both oracles with a similar historical situation. Thus we conclude that, like 3:1-3, the third oracle is also a response to one of the several lament rituals enacted upon the people's return from exile. However, this third response exhibits a closer association with the elements of the lament ritual in chs. 1 – 2 than do the other responses. The devastation which the returnees saw when they reached Jerusalem was overwhelming, and they immediately recalled the enemy which had brought such a situation about. Under the twin images of due punishment (vv. 9-13) and a return of the land's bounty (vv. 14-18), Joel comforts the returnees, assuring them of a bright future. At that time they will know again of Yahweh's protection and ever-caring presence. This will be true not only in their cultic life but also in the bounty of the land which makes that cultic life possible.

Oracle against the Nations, IV (3:19-21)

The final foreign nation oracle directs attention to two enemies, Egypt and Edom. For centuries Egypt had been an enemy of Israel, had in fact killed her most illustrious king, Josiah (2 Kgs. 23:29). Edom more recently, since 587 B.C., had taken on that identity. The oracle as a whole sets up a contrast between the enemies and Judah; the former will be devastated as Judah currently is (cf. 1:17), and the latter will enjoy permanent habitation.

The two enemy nations will be devastated (RSV "desolation," Heb. *shemamah*). This term is a favorite of Ezekiel as he recounts punishment to be meted out against Egypt in ch. 32 and against Edom in ch. 35 (cf. Obad. 10). Behind these and other foreign nation oracles rests the use of the term *desolation* in the lament psalms — see, for example, Ps. 40:14; 69:26; 79:7. In addition, *violence* (committed against God's people) is a term found often in these laments (Ps. 5:9; 74:20; 140:1).

Egypt and Edom are accused both of violence toward Judah (cf. Obad. 11) and of shedding "innocent blood" (v. 19b). Ps. 79:10 calls on Yahweh to avenge the bloodshed suffered by his people, so that we are aware of this expression in the liturgies of lament. One difficulty which the idea of innocent suffering raises here is that if the lament relates back at least partially to the events of 587 B.C., we have no grounds to argue that Judah suffered innocently; rather, all interpretations of that event by prophets such as Jeremiah, Ezekiel, and Deutero-Isaiah insist that the Exile was a long-overdue punishment. But one possible approach to the text ought not to be overlooked. The word *innocent*, when used to describe bloodshed, can refer to the brutal deaths of young children, those in the community who have been taken advantage of, that is, the victims of violence (cf. Ps. 106:38; Isa. 59:7). This would suggest that the evil with which the two nations here are charged is that of violating accepted standards of conduct and stooping to barbarism in their dealings with Judah. Even though in the past both served as agents for the carrying out of Yahweh's judgment of Judah, nevertheless they are still accountable to God for their barbaric conduct.

Throughout the OT, the judgment which Yahweh brings is directed against all humanity, whether it is in covenant relationship with him as Judah was, or related to him as creature is to Creator. All humanity stands in the latter relationship with him. As Paul recognizes in Rom. 1:18-20 and 2:12-15, those without knowledge of the divine law will be judged on the basis of whatever knowledge of moral value is available to them. Whatever the criterion, God's judgment will nevertheless be just, and it will be meted out against every form of evil and injustice.

The contrast in v. 20 lies in the bright future assured for Judah — permanent habitation will replace the present desolation. Such a long-term future is emphasized by parallel expressions in the verse, and by the two expressions "for ever" *(leʿolam)* and "to all generations" *(ledor wador)*. In addition, the latter expression provides the inclusion or "bracketing" device for the entire book of Joel — in 1:2 Joel spoke of the unprecedented calamity which had overtaken the land and suggested that it would be talked about from one "generation" *(dor)* to the next. In 3:20 he remarks that the new future will be enjoyed by all coming "generations." Thus into the future, alongside their present prosperity, will go the story of their earlier devastation. The Davidic covenant background to this promise is obvious, though like Isa. 55, Joel sees that relationship broadened from a promise given to the Davidic family to one which embraces all residents of the land.

The oracle concludes in v. 21 with a phrase about Yahweh avenging their blood and not clearing the guilty. It is a phrase of some difficulty in the original text. We may translate v. 21a literally as follows: "I declared innocent their blood (which) I did not declare innocent" (see RSV mg), with the possible meaning that a nation, Judah, which previously was guilty and deserving of punishment, has passed through the discipline of exile and now has a new beginning. As proof of that, Yahweh returns to Zion to tabernacle *(shakan)* or "dwell" with his people. The thought that God is ever present with us in and beyond our crises is a fundamental one in biblical theology. It is expressed so clearly in the young child Immanuel ("God with us"), the living sign given to King Ahaz (Isa. 7:14), and in the NT's application of that same name to Jesus in an attempt to illustrate his theological significance (Matt. 1:23).

The coupling of Egypt and Edom together in one oracle makes it difficult to identify one particular historical event as the setting for this response. But if we locate the book of Joel in a lament context after the Exile, it is most probable that the community in Jerusalem, still suffering shock at the sight of the devastation of their capital, railed in lament against those who had sought to bring harm upon God's chosen land and people. If this be so, then v. 20 takes on added significance as a defiant affirmation that despite the depressing sight of a broken Jerusalem, the nation will emerge to new prosperity. Once again, as Isaiah of Jerusalem maintained (cf. Isa. 2), Yahweh present in Zion is the guarantee of that better future.

The abiding presence of God with his people, a promise the Christian community identifies with Immanuel, is the ground of hope and assurance for all the faithful. Past, present, or future, "God with us" is the biblical message to those seeking comfort in an adverse world.

EXCURSUS: YAHWEH'S ACTIONS IN THE WORLD

Joel bases his words of comfort to Judah on the conviction that Yahweh is an active participant in world events. Like other prophets of the OT, Joel believes that it is not only possible to account for historical events in terms of what God does, but that it is necessary to do so. In the specific examples of the oracles of judgment against foreign nations, Joel sets forth the view that God *alone* will correct the injustices of the world.

We must see this emphasis on divine action against the background of Judah's plight, expressed in chs. 1 – 2 of the lament. Judah is in such desperate straits that it is totally dependent upon outside help, namely, from God. There is no recourse but to cry to God for deliverance and for the bringing to justice of those who caused such destruction. Thus Joel, in responding to the people's cry for help, indicates that Yahweh the compassionate will vindicate his justice; he alone can bring to judgment those who perpetrated the evil in question.

Perhaps it is because of the nation's inability to do anything for itself that Joel lays such an emphasis for "restoring the years" upon Yahweh. Certainly there are many situations in our personal lives, as well as in the wider setting, in which we feel unable to do anything to bring about a solution. To depend upon a compassionate God to come to our aid is our only hope. However, this is not to say that every situation is of that order. There is truth, therefore, in the suggestion that we are called to join God in his work in the world to effect salvation and deliverance, to bring hope and comfort to those in need. The latter course requires that we be sensitive to the way in which God is acting to bring about such healing. The special emphasis that Joel gives is that such a restoration of harmony lies ultimately in God's hands, not in ours. The Scriptures call us to love our "enemies" (Matt. 5:44), a term which in the OT laments is applicable to any kind of opposition, injustice, or difficulty. That we should

51

use a method other than that of love to deal with such crises flies in the face of this basic scriptural attitude (Prov. 25:21-22; Rom. 12:14-21). Those in situations of entrenched injustice and of oppression are not excepted from this, but are called to a peculiar reliving of the love manifested in Christ's own death and resurrection.

RHETORICAL FEATURES IN THE BOOK OF JOEL

1. INCLUSION OR "BRACKETING" DEVICE

– "generation" *(dor)* in 1:3 and 3:20
– reference to the four forms or stages of locust life (1:4; 2:25) binds together all the intervening material

2. KEYWORDS OR PHRASES

– "elders, all inhabitants of the land" (*zekenim, kol yoshebe ha'arets*, 1:2, 14)
– "wail" (*yalal*, 1:5, 11, 13)
– "strong" (*'atsum*, 1:6; 2:2, 5, 10)
– "gird on" (*hagar*, 1:8, 13)
– "cut off" (*karat*, 1:9, 16)
– "cereal offering" and "drink offering" (*minhah, nesek*, 1:9, 13; 2:14)
– "priest" and "minister" (*kohen, mesharet*, 1:9, 13; 2:17)
– "field" (*sadeh*, 1:10, 12, 19)
– "trees of the field" (*'atse hassadeh*, 1:12, 19)
– "perish" (*'amal*, 1:10, 12)
– "corn, grain" (*dagan*, 1:10, 17; 2:19)
– "wine and oil" (*tirosh weyitshar*, 1:10; 2:19, 24).
– "vine" and "fig tree" (*gephen, te'enah*, 1:7, 12; 2:22)
– "lament" and "fast" (*saphad, tsom*, 1:13, 14; 2:12-14, 15)
– "day of the LORD" (*yom yahweh*, 1:15; 2:1, 11, 31; 3:14)
– "joy and gladness" (*simhah wagil*, 1:16; 2:21, 23)
– "fire, flame" (*'esh, lahat, lahabah*, 1:19, 20; 2:3, 5)
– "cattle" (*behemah*, 1:18, 20)
– "pastures of the wilderness" (*ne'ot midbar*, 1:19, 20; 2:22)
– "tremble" (*ragaz*, 2:1, 10)
– "war" (*milhamah*, 2:5, 7; 3:9)
– "escape" (*peletah*, 2:3, 32)

— "reproach" (*herpah*, 2:17, 19)
— "send" (*shalah*, 2:19, 25; 3:13)

3. ASSONANCE

— 1:10, the verb "destroy" (*shadad*, Pual), and the noun "field" *(sadeh)*
— 1:15, the noun "destruction" *(shod)* and the divine name "the Almighty" *(shadday)*
— 1:10, 11, 12, 20, "fail" (*hobish*, Hiphil) and the similar sounding "dry up" (*yabash*)

4. THEMATIC ASSOCIATIONS

The "reversal" theme is a central literary device in 2:18-27 and 2:28 – 3:21. The sending of rain reverses the previous "drought" (2:23); abundance of food reverses the present shortage (2:24); destruction is replaced by new provisions (2:25); punishment of the nations is in the form of a reversal of what they have done to Judah so that it is now on their own heads (2:28 – 3:21). Thus Judah's anguish is reversed and becomes joy (2:21, 23).

5. CONTRASTING IMAGERY

The contrast "before" and "after" forms the framework around which the discussion in ch. 2 is constructed (2:3, 6, 10, 11, 14, 20). The contrast is used to picture the land before the crisis with the land after it, and to highlight what the nations leave behind, namely, destruction, over against what Yahweh leaves behind, namely, his blessing.

The above literary features indicate how closely together chs. 1 – 2 are woven. However, the most troublesome question histor–ically has been the relationship of 2:28 – 3:21 to the preceding material. The following list of literary elements, all of them key words or phrases, is concrete evidence for the unity of the total work.

— "day of the LORD" (*yom yahweh*, 1:15; 2:1, 11, 31; **3:14**)
— "sacred mountain" (*har qodesh*, 2:1; **3:17**)
— "darkness" (*hoshek*, 2:2; **2:31**)
— "escape" (*peletah*, 2:3; **2:32**)
— "war" (*milhamah*, 2:5, 7; **3:9**)
— the earth "shakes" (*ra'ash, ragaz*, 2:10; **3:16**)
— "sanctify . . . gather" (*qadash . . . qabats*, 1:14; 2:16; **3:2, 11**)

- "send away" (*rahaq*, 2:20; **3:8**)
- "know Yahweh" (*yada῾ yahweh*, 2:27; **3:17**)
- "pour out" (*shaphak*, 2:28; **3:19**)
- "generation(s)" (*dor*, 1:3; **3:20**)

QUOTATIONS IN THE BOOK OF JOEL

The following is a list of material generally recognized as quotations from other OT writers:

1:15	"alas for the day" (Ezek. 30:2-3)
	"the day of the LORD is near" (Ezek. 30:2-3; Obad. 15; Zeph. 1:7)
	"as destruction from the Almighty" (Isa. 13:6)
2:2	"day of darkness and gloom" (Zeph. 1:14-15)
2:6b	"in anguish, all faces grow pale" (Nah. 2:10)
2:10	"the stars withdraw their shining" (Isa. 13:10, 13)
2:11, 31	"the great and terrible day of the LORD" (Mal. 3:2; 4:5)
2:13b	"God is gracious, merciful, and slow to anger" (Jonah 4:2; Exod. 34:6; Ps. 86:15; 103:8; 145:8)
2:14a	"who knows whether he will turn and repent" (Jonah 3:9).
2:17	"where is their God?" (Ps. 79:10)
2:20	"the northerner" (Jer. 1:14-15; 4:6; 6:1, 22; Ezek. 38:6)
2:27, 3:17	"you shall know that I am the LORD" (Isa. 45:5, 6; Ezek. 38:23)
2:28	"I will pour out my spirit" (Isa. 44:3; Ezek. 39:29)
2:31	"before the great and terrible day comes" (Mal. 4:5)
2:32	"for in Mt. Zion will be those who escape" (Obad. 17)
3:1	"in those days and at that time" (Jer. 33:15; 50:4, 20)
3:2	"I will gather all nations" (Isa. 66:18; Zech. 14:2)
3:4, 7	"I will requite your deeds on your head" (Obad. 15)
3:8	"for the LORD has spoken" (Obad. 18)

3:9	"prepare war" (Jer. 6:4)
3:10a	"beat plowshares into swords" (reverses Isa. 2:4)
3:16	"the LORD roars from Zion" (Amos 1:2)
3:18	"mountains shall drip sweet wine" (Ezek. 47:1, 12; Amos 9:13)

BIBLIOGRAPHY

Ahlström, G. W. *Joel and the Temple Cult of Jerusalem*. Supplements to *Vetus Testamentum* 21 (Leiden: Brill, 1971).

Allen, L. C. *Joel, Obadiah, Jonah, Micah*. New International Commentary on the Old Testament (Grand Rapids: Eerdmans, 1976).

Anderson, B. W. *Out of the Depths* (New York: United Methodist Church Board of Missions, 1970).

Bewer, J. A. "Joel," in J. M. P. Smith, W. H. Ward, and J. A. Bewer. *A Critical and Exegetical Commentary on the Books of Micah, Zephaniah, Nahum, Habakkuk, Obadiah and Joel*. International Critical Commentary (Edinburgh: T. & T. Clark and New York: Scribner's, 1911).

Bright, J. *Jeremiah*. Anchor Bible (New York: Doubleday, 1965).

Childs, B. S. *Introduction to the Old Testament as Scripture* (Philadelphia: Fortress, 1979).

Credner, K. A. *Der Prophet Joel übersetzt und erklärt* (Halle: 1831).

Dennefeld, L. "Les problèmes du livre de Joël," *Revue des Sciences Religieuses* 6 (1926) 26-49.

Duhm, B. "Anmerkungen zu den zwölf Propheten," *Zeitschrift für die alttestamentliche Wissenschaft* 31 (1911) 184-88.

Eissfeldt, O. *The Old Testament: An Introduction*. Trans. P. R. Ackroyd (Oxford: Blackwell and New York: Harper & Row, 1968).

Elliger, K. "Ein Zeugnis aus der jüdischen Gemeinde im Alexanderjahr 332 v. Chr.," *Zeitschrift für die alttestamentliche Wissenschaft* 62(1950) 63-115.

Hayes, J. H. "The Usage of Oracles against Foreign Nations in Ancient Israel," *Journal of Biblical Literature* 87 (1968) 81-92.

Jepsen, A. "Kleine Beiträge zum Zwölfprophetenbuch," *Zeitschrift für die alttestamentliche Wissenschaft* 56 (1938) 85-96.

Kaiser, O. *Introduction to the Old Testament*. Trans. J. Sturdy (Oxford: Blackwell and Minneapolis: Augsburg, 1975).

Kapelrud, A. *Joel Studies* (Uppsala: Lundequist, 1948).

Miller, P. D. *Sin and Judgment in the Prophets*. Society of Biblical Literature Monograph Series 27 (Chico: Scholars Press, 1982).

Murray, R., "Prophecy and the Cult." In *Israel's Prophetic Tradition: Essays in Honour of Peter Ackroyd*. Ed. R. Coggins, A. Phillips, and M. Knibb (Cambridge: Cambridge University Press, 1982), 200-216.

Myers, J. M. "Some Considerations Bearing on the Date of Joel," *Zeitschrift für die alttestamentliche Wissenschaft* 74 (1962) 177-95.

Ogden, G. S. "Joel 4 and Prophetic Responses to National Laments," *Journal for the Study of the Old Testament* 26 (1983) 97-106.

Plöger, O. *Theocracy and Eschatology.* Trans. S. Rudman (Richmond: John Knox, 1968).

Robinson, T. H. and F. Horst. *Die Zwölf Kleinen Propheten.* Handbuch zum Alten Testament. 3rd ed. (Tübingen: Mohr, 1964).

Rothstein, J. W. *Einleitung in die Literatur des Alten Testaments* (1896).

Sellin, E. *Das Zwölfprophetenbuch.* Kommentar zum Alten Testament (Leipzig: Diechert, 1922).

Thompson, J. A. "The Book of Joel: Introduction and Exegesis." In *Interpreter's Bible.* Ed. G. Buttrick, et al. (Nashville: Abingdon, 1956) 6:729-60.

Vernes, M. *Le peuple d'Israël et ses espérances* (Paris: 1872).

Weiser, A. *Das Buch der zwölf Kleinen Propheten, I.* Das Alte Testament Deutsch (Göttingen: Vandenhoeck & Ruprecht, 1967).

Westermann, C. *Praise and Lament in the Psalms.* Trans. K. Crim and R. Soulen (Edinburgh: T. & T. Clark, 1965; repr. Atlanta: John Knox, 1981).

―――. "The Role of the Lament in the Theology of the Old Testament" (trans. R. Soulen), *Interpretation* 28 (1974) 20-38.

Wolff, H. W. *Joel and Amos.* Hermeneia. Trans. W. Janzen, et al. (Philadelphia: Fortress, 1977).

CALLING GOD'S PEOPLE
TO OBEDIENCE

A Commentary on the Book of
Malachi

RICHARD R. DEUTSCH

I dedicate this to Elisabeth Maria Deutsch-Erhardt,
my dear wife, my steady companion, counselor, and patient friend
for the past thirty years

CONTENTS

AUTHOR'S PREFACE

My love for the Hebrew Bible is the gift of my ancestors, many of whom have paid with their lives for being what they were, people of Jewish descent. Grandmother reading the Sabbath Eve prayers is one of my earliest memories. Study and teaching is the other root of this love. Gerhard von Rad inspired me with the desire to be able "to look over the shoulders" of those who wrote those records which make up our Bible. Many discussions with students and church members in Hong Kong and Burma have deepened and broadened my love for and my understanding of the Bible as a whole, and the prophets in particular. This exposition has gained greatly through the careful attention and friendly encouragement the series editors George A. F. Knight and Fredrick Holmgren were kind enough to give. Special gratitude is due to my son Christian, who originally put the manuscript on disk and introduced me to this way of writing.

RICHARD R. DEUTSCH

INTRODUCTION

"MALACHI": PERSONAL NAME OR TITLE?

The name Malachi may be the real name of a person. If it is, the
form "Malachi" is short for Malachiya, like other Northwest Semitic sentence-names, e.g., Abram, Abimelech, Zechariah. The last
syllable would then be a shortened form of Yahweh. Such a name
may be translated as "messenger of Yahweh," or "my messenger
is Yahweh." But it is more likely that Malachi is not a personal
name but a title, "my messenger" (i.e., "prophet"). For this is
what the word clearly means in 2:7 and 3:1. Since much of this
small collection of messages is styled as the direct speech of
Yahweh, the use of the title "my messenger" for the prophet who
delivered these messages is not at all surprising.

PLACE AND TIME OF ORIGIN

The contents of Malachi in some places are similar to portions
of Ezra, Haggai, Obadiah, and late material in Isaiah. This gives
us some clues as to the community to which "Malachi" belonged,
as well as to the time and place in which he lived. In this way we
may recognize that the problems referred to in Malachi were
problems common to the postexilic community in and around
Jerusalem, between 450 and 350 B.C.

However, it is difficult to determine the exact times of these
distinct situations in the community of Malachi that brought
about these problems. The section on Edom, 1:2-5, seems to refer
to events that occurred later than those predicted in Jer. 49;
Obad. 1-4; and Isa. 34; 63. Likewise the section on divorce,
2:13-14, deals with a problem similar to that mentioned in Ezra
9:2 – 10:17 and Neh. 13:23-30. The section on tithes, Mal. 3:6-12,
reminds us strongly of Hag. 1:7-11 and 2:16-19, though the latter
passages refer to a time before the rebuilding of the temple. This
means that as far as the subjects are concerned it is not difficult

to decide that the prophet who made these pronouncements in "Malachi" was part of the postexilic community in Jerusalem.

The approximate period in which his pronouncements were made may be deduced from the events referred to in Malachi and other texts. A more exact dating may occasionally suggest itself in some passages, but it must remain hypothetical. Generally speaking the time of Malachi was after the completion of the second temple (515 B.C.) and before the final breakdown of Persian rule in Palestine (the conquest of Palestine by Alexander the Great in 332 B.C.). One further clue to the dating of our book is the occurrence of a term of Mesopotamian origin for "governor" in 1:8. In most biblical instances this term refers to Persian administrators abroad; its use helps us to place the book in the period when Palestine was part of the Persian empire (see, e.g., Hag. 1:1, 14; Ezra 8:36; Neh. 2:7; Est. 3:12; 8:9).

THE STRUCTURE: REFLECTING ACTUAL DISPUTES?

The person who compiled the book of Malachi made use of a traditional style to give his book a characteristic form. The style of "prophetic dispute" was only one of several traditional ways in which prophets spoke to their people. We find it, e.g., in Deutero-Isaiah (40:27; 47:5-11; 49:3-4, 14-18), in Ezekiel (18:1-4, 25-29; 20:1-5), and in Haggai (passim). Malachi first quotes a word of Yahweh, then cites the response of the people as they either doubted or actually contradicted Yahweh's words. In addition, there is usually an exposition of those particular words, predictions, exhortations, warnings, or requests addressed to the people and the priests. Seven sections are styled in this manner, and each introduces a new subject: (a) 1:2-3, Esau and Jacob; (b) 1:6, honoring and/or despising the LORD's name: impaired sacrificial animals; (c) 1:12-13, profaning God's name: going back on one's vows; (d) 2:13-14, divorce; (e) 2:17, good and evil; (f) 3:6-7, tithes; (g) 3:13, retribution. One additional instance of a new subject, at 2:1-12, which deals with the responsibility of the Levitical priests, lacks this introduction.

THE BACKGROUND

What Was the Postexilic Jewish Community Like?

Two important sources of information on this community are the books of Ezra and Nehemiah. From both of these we can learn how strong and self-conscious were these Jews who had returned to Jerusalem from Babylonia. In their opinion, the true "Israel" was the community peopled by those who had gone through the Babylonian experience (see, e.g., Ezra 3:8; 6:16; 10:7-8; Neh. 8:17; 10:28-31).

However, we know that the majority of those who made up the postexilic Jewish community in Jerusalem and the surrounding area were persons who had never been away from their homeland. This fact must have caused numerous problems because the returnees claimed the right to leadership in the renewed community (see, e.g., Isa. 57:3-13; 65:1-9; Ezra 6:19-21; 7:1-14, 25-26; Neh. 8:1-8; 10:28-39). In the long run it meant of course that there were various viewpoints on religious and community subjects. While some teachings, such as circumcision and Sabbath, were considered basic by all, new teachings were being introduced. In fact the Torah, the Instruction of Moses, was itself brought back from Babylonia by the returnees (Ezra 7:6, 10, 14). In this form the Torah, i.e., the books of Genesis through Deuteronomy, was largely a product of the Exile. Some traditions, stories, and community rules contained in these books had been known in Israel since much earlier times, but the returnees' claim to absolute authority was new.

In Babylonia, the deported Judeans had to learn to sustain their religious life without the traditional framework of the temple and the cult. Hence new forms of the community's religious life had developed there. One of these was the institution of "scribes" (Ezra 7:1-6). Ezra himself was described in terms of what later Jewish rabbis were like (Ezra 7:10). Another such institution was the "assembly" of worshipers (see, e.g., Neh. 8:1-12, 13; 9:1; Ezra 10:7-9). This was later known as a "synagogue" in the Greek-speaking diaspora.

When some of these new forms of the community's religious life were brought back to Judea by repeated waves of returnees (who began returning at ca. 538 B.C., when Cyrus issued his famous "edict"), they surely had a limiting effect on the former authority of the temple and its traditional cult (see, e.g., Neh. 10; Sir. 51:23; and Martin Hengel, *Judaism and Hellenism*, 1:79; 2:54, n.165). After the Persian empire had given way to the Macedonian Alexander the Great and his successors, the Jewish community was faced with a new and dangerous situation: strict obedience to the Torah was confronted with the demand for tolerance toward the Hellenistic cultural influence. This was coupled with questions of political alignment, of how much cooperation with non-Jews was possible, and ultimately, whether passive or active military resistance to the foreign overlords was called for (see, e.g., 1 Macc. 1:41-64; 2:1-18; 2 Macc. 3–4; and Hengel, *Judaism and Hellenism*, 1:78).

During Maccabean and Roman times, the community which is known to have existed at Qumran originated out of protest against "the Judaism of their time, which they considered wicked and corrupt" (see Geza Vermes, *The Dead Sea Scrolls in English*, 16). Their teaching differed in many details from that of official Judaism, yet they were convinced of being the only true Israel (see, e.g., 1QH 7; Vermes, *The Dead Sea Scrolls*, 161-63). Jews living "dispersed" among non-Jews (in Egypt, Syria, and later in Greek-ruled nations) always had to struggle with problems arising out of their loyalty to their tradition, which was in opposition to the demanded tolerance of non-Jewish, mainly Greek culture (see, e.g., Hengel, *Judaism and Hellenism*, 1:65-78).

The Problems within Malachi's Community

All eight sections of the book have the literary forms of "instruction" and "exhortation" in common. The contents suggest certain situations that seem to have been the reasons for such words being spoken. In general these might be summarized thus:

1. An unexpected revival of Edomite strength and influence, threatening the Jewish community. Edom, south of Judah, was Judah's traditional enemy.

2-3. The appearance of two problems in the sacrificial cult at the temple in Jerusalem, with the resulting offense of "the breaking of vows."

4. Lack of teaching causing people to commit offenses like divorcing Jewish women and marrying non-Jewish women.

5. Confusing "right" and "wrong," another result of the lack of teaching concerning moral issues.

6. Complaints about poverty; the complaints are then turned into exhortations.

7. Ignoring traditional demands of faith, and the threat of retribution for wrong and immoral deeds.

The additional section 2:1-12 reprimands the Levitical priests for neglecting their duty to teach the people.

Some Conclusions Concerning the Background of the Book

The problems which induced the messenger to speak up make it appear that in this community the influence of the "returnees" was still relatively weak. Although "teaching" and consequently obedience to the demands of the Torah are prominent, the position taken by the "messenger" is not as radical as, e.g., in the books Ezra and Nehemiah.

THE THEOLOGICAL BACKGROUND OF MALACHI

The "messenger's" words were intended to reprimand the people and the leaders of the community for the lack of sincerity in their worship and their lives. In many ways his views can be compared with those of prophets like Haggai and Zechariah, or of reformers like Ezra and Nehemiah. The basis of his criticism was the Torah. Many Bibles render the Hebrew word *torah* as "law" (see Mal. 4:4). "Law" can be easily misunderstood. One example of such misunderstanding is Paul's controversy in Rome (see Rom. 2:12-29; 3:1-26, esp. v. 24), and James's seemingly contradictory conviction (see Jas. 1:22-25; 2:14-26). A more appropriate translation which also agrees with Jewish understanding and usage is "instruction."

Malachi's group, however, did not have these problems. The early Jewish community at Jerusalem tried to *live* according to their God's will. "Faith" and "actions" cannot be separated; the Torah assures people that they are accepted by God and teaches them to live within his love. We do not know for certain what the Torah of Malachi's time contained, whether it was as comprehensive as that of later times, comprising all five "Books of Moses." But from the contents of Malachi we can see that it must have contained instructions concerning vows, sacrifices, divorce, morality, tithes, and retribution, as well as the traditional stories about Jacob and Esau. It certainly also contained Deut. 33:8-11 (about the Levitical priests), because Mal. 2:1-9 appears to refer directly to it.

The Central Theological Concern

From the above it can be concluded that the Torah, at the time of Malachi, was already the most important guideline for the worship and the life of the Jewish community. Its instructions and demands were directed at all Jews alike. Nevertheless, according to Malachi the priests had a special responsibility to teach and guide the members of the community. Hence the "additional section" 2:1-12, in the middle of this short book, takes on special importance. Its difference in literary form and emphasis from the rest of the book appear to stress the central theological concern of the compiler/editor of Malachi. The "Torah"

71

is not simply the "instruction of the priests" (see, e.g, Deut. 17:11; Hag. 2:11); it conveys the true will of God. To teach such "Torah" and thus truly to "instruct" people in how to live according to God's will is the task of priests as genuine "messengers of the LORD" (Mal. 2:5-7). Only such "instruction" can become an effective correction of the problems in the life of the community.

The Torah Is Life-centered

The Torah theology underlying the ideas and intentions of Malachi most certainly is not an abstract dogmatic structure. First, it is based on a sincere commitment to God. Second, and because of this, its urgent demands concern the vital interhuman relationships as much as matters related to the temple. Thus remaining faithful to one's first wife, preserving law and order, and bringing justice to bear for the defenseless are as important as being honest to God by offering proper sacrifices and standing by one's vows (see, e.g., 1:6-14; 2:13-16; 3:5). Like any human theology, however, Torah theology could not escape the fate of becoming one-sided, restrictive, and rigid, although such changes are not always due to the passage of time. Like other "late" books (e.g., Jonah and parts of Trito-Isaiah), Malachi reveals a universalistic outlook (1:11), and the reprimand on "divorce" (2:13-16) seems to have a different emphasis from the exclusive "purity" dogma of Ezra and Nehemiah (see, e.g., Ezra 9:2; 10:2-4, 19; Neh. 10:30; 13:23ff.). The latter demands were probably more the result of the dogmatic pressure of the Jewish community at Babylon than the result of an actual need within the Judean community (see, e.g., Isa. 58:1-12).

REDACTIONS, OR TRANSMISSION BY STUDY AND ADAPTATION

Biblical books were preserved and handed down primarily by being studied, copied, and adapted to new situations for continued use in the community. This is true for most ancient books, like the Gilgamesh Epic, the Enuma Elish (the Mesopotamian creation story), as well as for Job, the material in the Pentateuch, and the section Joshua to Kings. In the same manner it would probably be correct to say that Malachi has gone through many hands and has been added to in one way or another. It may be helpful to consider why at some stage certain comments were added at all.

1. Possibly "repetition": this would indicate a time when peo-

ple had a different understanding of the subject matter, e.g., 2:16b as compared with v. 15b.

2. Comments interrupting a coherent sequence of thought: these suggest marginal notes which were later copied as part of the text, e.g., 2:7.

3. Added theological explanations, intended to change the meaning of a passage, e.g., 3:1b, "the messenger of the covenant."

A further example is Mal. 4:5-6, which the editor added when the collection of the prophets was put together.

"Malachi" Originally Part of Another Book?

It has been claimed that Malachi is an anonymous collection of material comparable to Zech. 9–14, and that only the word "Malachi" prevented its inclusion in Zechariah. But the argument concerning the word itself (whether name or title) carries no weight.

Like Zechariah, Malachi may have been handled as "unattached prophecies." This could be concluded from the quotation in Matt. 27:9, where Zech. 11:12-13 is attributed to Jeremiah. Hence in Matthew's day Zechariah may have been a collection attached to Jeremiah.

Only the content and structure of Zech. 1–8, 9–14, and Malachi permit us to come to some general conclusions as to why Malachi was not simply included in Zechariah. Zech. 1–8 contains a series of personal visions and auditions, most of which refer to the time preceding the completion of the second temple (515 B.C.). The first part of Zech. 9–14 (i.e., 9:1–11:3) contains threats against nations that were once ruled by David: they shall once more "belong" to God (9:1). There are promises for a peaceful future of "Israel," despite "your sons, O Greece" (9:13) (i.e., Alexander the Great or his successors who conquered and ruled Mesopotamia, Syria-Palestine, and Egypt after 332 B.C.). There is the further promise in which God declares: "I will . . . gather them in. . . . Though I scattered them among the nations" (see 10:8-12). The rest (11:4–14:21) contains various oracles concerning "that day" (see, e.g., 12:3).

Malachi is very different from the above; it is laid out as a series of discussions, and its contents refer to actual problems within the postexilic Jewish communities at Jerusalem and in Judea.

While the exact dates of individual passages in Zech. 9–14 may be disputable, the reference to "Greece" points to the earliest possible date of the final redaction, i.e., the end of the 4th cent.

B.C. This is certainly later than Malachi. Hence Malachi is sure to have been added as a separate book in its own right.

DIFFERENCES IN CHAPTERS AND VERSES

The RSV and other English versions follow the numbering used in the LXX and the Vulgate. Thus 4:1-6 corresponds to 3:19-24 of the MT.

CHAPTER 1

THE HEADING: GOD'S MESSENGER (1:1)

Verse 1 actually begins with a double heading, first "Oracle," then "The Word of the LORD to Israel by Malachi." Perhaps the two may be combined as in the RSV (but see Zech. 9:1 and 12:1). In Hab. 1:1 and many other instances, however, "oracle" is the subject of the sentence, and so no problem arises. "Problem" is too strong a word: the double heading only shows the process of compiling and editing. "Oracle" was placed at the beginning as a kind of classifier, i.e., to inform the reader what kind of text he was going to read.

Concerning the word "Malachi," the RSV adds a footnote, "my messenger." The LXX has a variant reading, "his messenger." It does not interpret "Malachi" as a personal name, but this does not prove it was not one. In the Bible the figure of the "angel of the LORD your God" is very important. The word translated as "messenger" is the same as that rendered "angel." In this way the title/name "messenger" with the possessive "my" carries important suggestive meanings for the reader in ancient and in modern times. For a number of important events in the OT and the NT are described with this figure playing a prominent role. For example, "the angel of the LORD your God" is mentioned twice in the Hagar stories (Gen. 16:7ff.; 21:17). This figure is even more significant in the description of the Exodus (Exod. 14:19), the entry into Canaan (Exod. 23:20, 23; 33:2), and the revelation to Moses (Exod. 3:2; Acts 7:30). It should be noted, however, that the use of the term "angel" is usually a method of avoiding speaking of God directly as a person.

In the LXX we also find an additional clause, "you ought to take this to heart"; this may have been inspired by Hag. 2:15, 18 (cf. *BHS*).

The use of "Israel" here is similar to that in Deutero-Isaiah and Ezekiel. In most passages in these books the meaning of "Israel" is no longer purely national or geographic, but theological: the "people of God." Within the Jewish community of post-exilic times, the idea of "Israel" was nevertheless limited to comprise persons of Jewish descent who consciously lived according to the religious traditions. Although Jewish descent remained one important requirement, it was never exclusive. But already in the Judaism of the postexilic period an exclusive viewpoint was advocated, for example, by Ezra and Nehemiah (see, e.g., Ezra 9:12; 10:2-4, 19; Neh. 10:30; 13:23ff.). However, it was not without opposition. The book of Jonah, Isa. 42:1-4; 49:6; and 56:1-8 are some examples of a more universalistic outlook. In the diaspora Judaism became a missionary religion, as we see from the number of proselytes and "devout" men and women mentioned in the NT (see, e.g., Acts 2:5; 6:5; 10:2; 13:50).

As Hengel points out (*Judaism and Hellenism*, 1:307), however, Israel could never quite rid itself of its "national" implication: "to become a Jew was never simply a religious action; it was always also a political decision: on his conversion the Gentile became a member of the Jewish 'ethnos'."

Romans 11, a passage dating back to early Christian times, bears witness to a very open attitude which included both Jew and Gentile as members of "Israel." Here Paul takes up the question of God's intention of salvation for all humanity — though it is very important for him to include "his people" also (11:1-2). Other passages explain the task of God's people. For example, in Isa. 49:6 it is God's purpose "that my salvation may reach to the end of·the world." Paul states that "through their trespass salvation has come to the Gentiles" (Rom. 11:11). These two passages deal with different situations: on the one hand, Deutero-Isaiah wishes to encourage the deported Judeans to recognize their task among the Babylonians; on the other hand, Paul writes to Gentile Christians who have been having difficulties in sorting out their own position in relation to the Jews. Rom. 11:17-21 thus represents an important statement: in God's work of salvation no one ought to be arrogant!

ESAU AND JACOB: A PARABLE OF GOD'S LOVE FOR "ISRAEL" (1:2-5)

The stories about Esau and Jacob in Genesis had already expressed God's preference for Jacob/Israel; moreover, this is clearly also the opinion put forward here in the statement " 'I have loved you,' says the LORD," and in the critical objection of those to whom Malachi spoke, "How hast thou loved us?"

In order to understand the meaning of "love of God" we might look somewhat closer at the two main strands of OT traditions on this subject:

1. Yahweh's love for Israel is an important theme in a tradition which links Hosea (3:1; 11:1; 14:5) with Jeremiah (31:3) and Deuteronomy (7:8, 12-13; 10:15; 23:5). The Hebrew word for "love" *('ahab)* with God as its subject occurs otherwise mostly in later passages (e.g., Isa. 41:8; 43:4). Verse 2 may be understood along this line of thought.

2. But a second group of traditions speaks of God's love in a different manner. The main themes are "Zion" and "David." Here the word "to choose" *(bahar)* is of basic importance (see, e.g., Ps. 78:68-70; 87:2; 132:13; 2 Sam. 6:21; Deut. 12:5; etc.).

One important difference between these two types of tradition must be noted. While the second *emphasizes the evidence of God's love*, the first *demands that the people of God show, on their part, evidence of their love for God* (Deut. 6:5). It will also be found that both types of "love" are often used with equivalents. In the second type God's love is seen as his "faithfulness" to his oaths, his covenant, and his promises (Deut. 7:8; cf. 4:31; Ps. 89:49; 105:8-11). But in the first type this love is understood as "loyalty" *(hesed)* (see, e.g., Hos. 6:6; Jer. 2:2-3). An interesting parallel to this last point, and particularly close to Deuteronomy, is the terminology in a Vassal Treaty of Esarhaddon (7th cent. B.C.) that repeatedly demands the absolute loyalty of the vassals to the overlord. Note that the actual term used there is "love"! (see *ANET*, 534-41).

At this point we may conclude that in Mal. 1:2 "love" *('ahab)* has the quality of "choose." Amos 3:2 expresses the same by "You only have I known." Hence in the light of the above, "love" means that God has "chosen" Jacob to serve God's purpose. Consequently in v. 3 "hate" *(sana')* must mean that Esau was "useless" for God's purpose.

The Love of God in Malachi's Community

"How hast thou loved us?" This question shows the direction of popular concern. The people looked for evidence of God's love. In former times it had been generally expected that this love would be evident in the greatness of their king and in peace for the people (2 Sam. 7:1, 8-9). Consequently this question proves that the old expectations were still present.

Further Developments in Judaism

Some of the passages referred to in the two traditions above date from the period of transition from what in the strict sense of the word is "Old Testament," to what is in fact the beginning of "Judaism." Generally speaking this transition began during the Exile in Babylon. After the downfall of Judah, the end of the Davidic dynasty, and the destruction of the first temple, ancient Israelite religious tradition and new Jewish theological thinking were both present. This is made very apparent in Trito-Isaiah, who flourished ca. 536-522 B.C. (see G. A. F. Knight, *The New Israel*).

It may often be neglected or denied, but there is little doubt that "Judaism" began during the time of the Exile. Of course, changes do not occur overnight. People living in different places will change their way of thinking to different extents and will be influenced by new ideas in varying degrees. The experiences in Palestine affected the people's way of thinking, as did the deportation to Babylon of a large number of Judeans. Those who returned to Jerusalem and Judea before, with, or after Nehemiah and Ezra will each have theologized in their own way because of what they had lived through. Their faith, hopes, and consequently their teachings were affected by these experiences (see, e.g., Neh. 1:2; 13:23).

However, culture, and in particular religious traditions, survive all sorts of changes of historical circumstances. (This phenomenon can be observed throughout the Bible.) Consequently a great variety of convictions is to be found in many passages from the period of the Exile and afterward. Some are closer to the preexilic prophetic tradition (see, e.g., Isa. 40 – 55; 56 – 66; Haggai; Zechariah). Others clearly advocate new teachings and standards (see, e.g., Ezra and Nehemiah). Some passages in the OT clearly protest against some of the hardening and narrowness evident in these "new teachings" (see, e.g., Jonah and passages in Trito-Isaiah). Another group of texts, from a later period, shows that in times of extreme desperation, people looked forward to God's miraculous salvation (see, e.g., Isa. 24 – 27; Daniel).

Many other texts in the OT also bear witness to the stubborn continuation of ancient traditions in the midst of the adaptation and development of convictions that took place during subsequent periods, up to and including postexilic times. One important spiritual and intellectual movement of this kind is associated with the book of Deuteronomy, which brought its influence to bear on many parts of the OT (e.g., Genesis through 2 Kings and Jeremiah). This reform-oriented movement originated in Israel, the northern part of the (then) divided country, probably during the time of Hosea. Its first achievement was the compilation of an (older) version of the book of Deuteronomy. After the end of the northern kingdom of Israel, this book was brought down into Judah in its original or already adapted form. It was undoubtedly an older version of the "law book" that was found in the temple at the time of King Josiah (2 Kgs. 22 – 23), and the one referred to by Jeremiah (see, e.g., Jer. 8:8). Another body of material with an even longer history is "priestly tradition." Within priestly families, not only rules and customs related to the cult in the temple were handed down, but a whole theology. The influence this tradition had is evident in Gen. 1 as well as in the book of Leviticus, Ezek. 40 – 48, and in many other passages of later times (see, e.g., 1 Chr. 1 – 9; 23 – 27; Ezra 2; 8; 10; Neh. 11 – 12; Hag. 1:10-14).

The actual features of the new theological developments during and after the Exile can only be briefly outlined here. Their emphases vary a great deal. Some of them may be summarized as follows:

1. God's concern for Zion/Jerusalem (e.g., compare Pss. 132 and 46, from ancient times, with Isa. 31:4-5; 37:33-35; and further with 26:1-3; 33:20; 49:14-18; 51:3; 62:1-5; 65:18-19; 66:10-11; Zeph. 3:14-18; Zech. 2:10; 9:9)

2. God remembering "David," the "ideal king" (Messiah) (e.g., compare 1 Kgs. 11:4, 6, 9-13; 14:7-8 with the symbol "branch" in Isa. 11:1; Jer. 23:5; 33:15; Zech. 3:8-9; 6:12; "king" in Isa. 32:1; 33:17; "David" in Hos. 3:5; Ezek. 34:23-24; 37:24-25; Isa. 55:3b-4)

3. God's unfailing love for the people (e.g., compare Jer. 3:14-18; 33:25-26 with Isa. 40:1-2; "election," the "chosen people" in Exod. 19:6; Isa. 41:8-9; 49:7; 65:9, 22; Neh. 9:7-8)

4. The importance of the Torah and its interpretation — the Babylonian influence (e.g., compare Deut. 6:4-8; 31:9-13, 24-26; 2 Kgs. 23:25 with Ezra 7:6; Neh. 8:1-11; 9:13-14; Ezra 3:2).

5. Sabbath and circumcision as important "signs of the covenant" (see, e.g., Jer. 17:21-22; Ezek. 20:12, 20; Isa. 56:2, 4, 6; 58:13; Neh. 13:15-21; "circumcision," Gen. 17:9-11; Josh. 5:2-7).

How these thoughts and ideas developed can be seen especially well in some of the later biblical and postbiblical writings, e.g., Haggai, Zechariah, Ezra, Nehemiah, later passages in Isaiah, Daniel, the Apocrypha, and the Dead Sea Scrolls as well as Malachi. Some of the relevant words have changed in meaning when compared with writings of the preexilic period. This applies especially to the theological meaning of terms like "Zion," "Israel," "David," and in their religious value to people living in those later times. It can be observed that terms such as these have lost almost all their original "historical" significance and have changed to represent "ideals" instead. Formally speaking, of course, they still represent historical realities such as "Jerusalem," "King David," "the people of Israel," etc., but their actual meaning to ordinary people, e.g., in Malachi's time, was very different. Such terms had by then come to point to a hope and to an ardent longing for its fulfillment. This can also be found in later passages of Isaiah (e.g., 25:6-8; 26:1-6; 27:1-6; 33:17-22; 65:17-25), and in Daniel (e.g., 2:44-45; 7:13-27; 12:1-3). The Apocrypha — 2 Esdras (e.g., 2:10-14, 18-22, 33-48; also chs. 10; 12), Tobit (e.g., 13:15-18), Baruch (5:1-9), and Sirach (e.g., 47:1-11; 49:4) — show the same development. Some hymns in the Dead Sea Scrolls (e.g., 1QH 10; 11; 22; 23; see Vermes, *The Dead Sea Scrolls*, 168ff.) also make the same point.

Early Christian writers in the NT quite naturally depended on previous Jewish theological ideas and patterns of thought. In an overall Christian setting these of course again changed their meaning and took on a more distinctly Christian identity (see, e.g., Rom. 10; 1 Pet. 2:4-10; Rev. 21:2-26).

Conclusions

Later piety, Jewish and Christian alike, combined both kinds of "love"-concepts with varying emphases at different times (see, e.g., the Prayer of Manasseh in the Apocrypha, and Jas. 2). To come back to Malachi and his community, in postexilic times the Jews in Jerusalem were still struggling to understand in their own personal and communal life-experience what God's love was all about. Their immediate concern was the presence and the future of those who had returned from exile. Back in the land of their fathers they now found themselves surrounded by people whom they experienced as "hostile." These "people of the land" were, in their view, different culturally and religiously because they had stayed behind, or had been affected by foreign influences. But quite obviously the "returnees" had also changed during their long exile in Babylon. Apart from formal differences between these two groups of people who could still trace their common background, Malachi's contemporaries also had to deal with

strangers who were trying to prevent the reestablishment of a
political community of Judeans (Ezra 3 – 4; Neh. 4; 6).

The Test Case, Edom (1:3-5)

To the Jews, the Edomites were apparently a kind of measure of
God's love for them. The critical response "How hast thou loved
us?" may refer to past events. Obadiah (vv. 11 – 14) describes in
detail how the Edomites had broken all the unwritten rules of
human relationships (see also Amos 1 – 2). This question could
also allude to the possible danger of a new attack by an Edom
that was regaining her strength. From the historical books we
gather that the relationship between the "brothers" Esau and
Jacob had always been very bad. But usually we hear only of the
harsh treatment which the Edomites received at the hands of
Judah and her kings, e.g., David (2 Sam. 8:12-14) and Amaziah
(2 Kgs. 14:8). The predictions in Isa. 34:5-17, as well as in Obadiah and elsewhere (Isa. 63; Jer. 49), point in the same direction.

Looking back now, we may nevertheless conclude that it was
their loyal love for God, practiced through spiritual commitment
to their faithful God, which helped the people of God, both Jewish
and later Christian communities, to survive through times of
terrible oppression and suffering. Yet they would surely praise
God's loyalty *(hesed)* as the cause of their survival (see, e.g., Pss.
124; 126; 136).

Hence we can conclude that this question which the Jews put
to God once again meant that, from the point of view of their
own expectations, Judah's dominance over Edom would be seen
as a sign of God's continued preference of love for Judah.

3-4 Contemporary Jews certainly understood Edom's devastation by the Babylonians and the Nabatean Arabs as God's dislike
for Edom. The word "hate" should not be taken in its full modern
force in this instance (e.g., Deut. 22:13; Judg. 14:16), although
this meaning is also possible (e.g., Gen. 37:4). Here, again from
the standpoint of the people in Judea, "hate" and "love" indicate
God's different attitude toward Edom and Israel (see at v. 2).

Instead of "jackals," the NEB has "lodging," and the JB "pasture"; however, the RSV translates the MT correctly and no
change is necessary.

At this instance no cause is mentioned for God's anger at
Edom. In the minds of Malachi and his countrymen, however,
it could only have been what is described by Obadiah in vv.
10-14: Edom's "violence done" to his "brother Jacob" (v. 10), that

he "stood aloof" (v. 11), that he "gloated . . . rejoiced over the people of Judah . . . boasted in the day of distress" (v. 12), that he "entered the gate of my people . . . looted his goods" (v. 13), and that he "stood at the parting of the ways to cut off his fugitives" (v. 14).

5 It cannot be overlooked that this divine anger and its result were a cause of joy and praise. To those people who had great difficulties in settling down in their fatherland once again, the fate of Edom certainly was a sign of God's continued faithfulness to Israel.

HONORING OR DESPISING GOD'S NAME (1:6-11)

6a This section begins with a question posed in the form of a parable. The pattern son-father/servant-master is followed immediately by its application in the first person. God responds: "If then I am a father . . . if I am a master . . . ?" The idea of God as "father" of Israel, even of humankind, is as old as humankind itself. But the meaning of this term is not as straightforward as might be expected. It does not always indicate a physical relationship. The abbot (i.e., actually "father") is head of a monastic community. In a similar manner leaders or heads of prophetic communities seem to have been called "father" (e.g., 2 Kgs. 2:12; 6:21; cf. the title "sons of the prophets" in 4:1; 6:1; etc.). In the Ugaritic text Krt, El bears the title "father of mankind" (I:37, etc.; see J. Gray, *The Legacy of Canaan*, 159). Accordingly, whenever Yahweh is called "father" or Israel "son" we have to bear this in mind (Deut. 32:6; cf. 1:31; see also Hos. 11:1, 3; Jer. 31:9b). Along the same lines Deutero-Isaiah and Trito-Isaiah regard God as Israel's creator or maker (see, e.g., 43:1; 44:24; 54:5; 64:8; see also Mal. 2:10), rather than as her "begetter" — and certainly not in terms of the "word" in John's Gospel (1:1-4).

6b-8 By means of the parable the priests are directly addressed. The link with the parable is obviously the parallel use of "honor" and "fear"/"despise my name," for those determine the emphasis of the whole section leading up to v. 11. The term "fear" is translated by "respect" in the JB. In fact, the quality of "fear" in the OT includes the positive value of "respect," but this still cannot represent the whole concept. Certainly the fear of God means real "dread," but used with a positive meaning. For example, Deut. 4:34 ("terrors"; cf. 26:8; 34:12; Jer. 32:21) uses this term in praising God for the salvation from Egypt. This "salvation" was the positive effect of the "fear of God." Also in other passages "salvation" is the common denominator (Isa. 8:12-13; Ps. 9:20; 76:11). This shows that the writers had a positive understanding of the "fear of God," namely, as the cause of Israel's salvation. This is further supported by the use of a related Hebrew word, also meaning "fear," in the so-called Wisdom literature (see, e.g., Ps. 111:10; 119:38; Job 28:28; Prov. 1:7; 8:13).

Deuteronomy is a good illustration of what is meant by this double request of "fear"/"respect" and "love." The best example is the *Shema* (Deut. 6:4-9) and its amplifications (Deut. 10:12-13; 11:18-22). Passages such as these characterize "love" as active "loyalty." In this sense this word "love" in Deuteronomy is close to a legal and political use in the Vassal Treaties of Esarhaddon (see *ANET,* 534-41, and above at v. 2). Such loyalty depends on "fear." However, biblical "love" and "fear of God" are in fact very different. God is not a cruel "overlord" who enforces "loyalty" at the pain of military aggression. "Fear" and "love" of this God are much rather a willing devotion to him of whom it is said "the LORD loves you" (see, e.g., Deut. 7:6-8; cf. 4:37; 9:5). His oath and covenant are based on such mutual devotion (see, e.g., Deut. 5:10; 7:9-11; 11:1, 13). Matt. 22:37-40 precisely reflects the Jewish standpoint. It is also easily recognizable in the "Ten Words" (Exod. 20:1-17; Deut. 5:6-21). Here and elsewhere the love of fellow human beings is emphasized. In actual "respect" and "love" toward others the sincerity of a person's love of God can be recognized (see, e.g., Rom. 13:10; Gal. 5:14; Jas. 2:8; 1 John 4:20-21).

Verse 6 ends by quoting another doubtful recourse of those addressed, "How have we despised thy name?" The term "name" deserves some reflection. The so-called Deuteronomistic School, which compiled the book of Deuteronomy and most of the books Joshua – Kings, uses "the name" to refer to God's presence in the temple (see, e.g., Deut. 12:5, 11, 21; 14:23; 1 Kgs. 8:29-30).

Such evidence points to a development of the understanding of "God." Earlier, people still unquestioningly followed a more anthropomorphic way of thinking and expression whereby God was spoken of and described as a human being (see, e.g., Gen. 3:8; 11:5; 18:1-8). A first step beyond this way of thinking was the replacement of "God" by "the angel of the LORD" (see, e.g., Gen. 16:7-13, esp. v. 13; 21:17 with both side by side). A further step is represented in 1 Kgs. 8:27: "will God indeed dwell on earth?" It was in fact what we would now call a breakthrough in the understanding of "immanence" and "transcendence."

This also explains other instances where "name" received special emphasis (see, e.g., Ps. 29:2; 66:2; 96:8). The present practice of some Jews to say *hashem* (i.e., "the name") instead of "God" probably stems from the same kind of thinking. The whole matter is, of course, much more complicated. These developments were also influenced by the postexilic tendency to protect the believers from any kind of sin, e.g., against the command in Exod. 20:7, "You shall not take the name of the LORD your God in vain." While we tend not to take names too seriously, ancient people had a very different attitude toward names. In the ancient view, as in many non-Western cultures today, a name expressed the character of a person or object, it might even embody the "power" of a person, his "mana" to use the Polynesian term. This view is retained in some of our fairy tales, where the knowledge of the "name" gives power over its bearer (cf. Judg. 13:17-18).

Are Only the Priests Responsible? (1:7-10)

7-8a   This section criticizes a questionable practice in the cult at the temple; hence, it is addressed to the priests. Priests, however, offer just such sacrifices as are brought to the temple by the people. Yet the priests are made responsible for mistakes that ordinary people make. We are hereby reminded of Mal. 2:8 and Hos. 4:6. The detailed description of what kinds of animals were brought and sacrificed strengthens the impression that even though the priests were responsible, the people were not without guilt. The rules about sacrifices apply to both. We are once more reminded of the section 2:1-12 and of its great importance for the whole composition of the material in Malachi; it outlines the responsibility of the priests toward the people of God.

However, the "messenger's" critique can be understood and explained as addressed to the priests and the ordinary people, both of whom are required to obey the Torah. For details on sacrificial animals see Lev. 22:19-25. Deut. 15:21 summarizes this rule, addressing it not to the priests but to the people as a whole.

8b-10   This impressive exhortation does not intend to put down, but rather to convince and to change attitudes considered to be wrong. The last clause leads back to the beginning of this section (cf. v. 6), summing up its main point.

Claims to Jewish Absolutism? (1:11)

Most commentaries consider this verse difficult. Some think it was added later, as an effort to express some hope for the future of the oppressed Jewish people. Others believe it comments on Jewish communities in the Diaspora, or even on rival Jewish cults in Egypt and the Samaritan temple. W. Rudolph *(Maleachi)* rightly stresses v. 11 as an integral part of Mal. 1. Three times the "name" is mentioned: once in respect of sacrifices offered to it and twice praising its greatness "among the nations." With these references to the "name," v. 11 is closely linked to the preceding and the following sections.

The statement "and in every place incense is offered to my name, and a pure offering" creates the greatest difficulty. At least since the time of King Josiah (ca. 622 B.C.; see 2 Kgs. 23) it was official religious policy that sacrifices could be offered only at the temple *in Jerusalem*. There were probably two reasons for this policy: (1) By doing so, the power of the government at Jerusalem was increased, because people had to come to Jerusalem for all important religious activities, and these could thus be better controlled. (2) The religious reform party, perhaps a forerunner of the so-called Deuteronomists, pushed for action against possible or actual worship of non-Israelite deities (see, e.g., Deut. 12; 2 Kgs. 22–23). This move, together with already existing strong interests in a centralized administration which would fully control everything, helped to produce the image of "absolutism." This represents a religious view in which the God of Israel in Jerusalem is the only true God—thus, so to speak, "tying" this God to Jerusalem. With regard to this view it has to be borne in mind that every ancient people considered its god the mightiest, most important, and sometimes even the "only god." Linked to this ideology is the conviction that particular nations or people had been specially created or chosen by their god (see, e.g., Judg. 11:24; Isa. 10:10-11; Hos. 8:14; 9:10).

After the Exile this type of conviction, together with the vital interest of leaders seeking to keep the people together (by preventing a gradual absorption of Jews by other nations) increased the power of this religious-theological absolutism. To be sure, however, this is only one of several views or convictions in the OT. When prophets like Amos, Isaiah, and Jeremiah spoke to the people they often tried to correct this view of a "people apart" (see, e.g., Amos 1:3–2:12; 9:7; Isa. 10:5-7; 20; Jer. 25:15-29). They wanted them to see all of humanity together, and the God of Israel as the God of the whole world. But even they would not deny the special relationship between this God and Israel. They emphasized it as a special responsibility (Amos 3:2). The socalled Servant-of-Yahweh poems (Isa. 42; 49; 50; 52–53) emphasize this point: Israel and Judah are described as God's servants, bringing God's truth and justice (i.e., his salvation) to all people. Theologically this is a very interesting view of the "diaspora"! It refers to Judeans and Israelites who were exiled and to those who moved away from Palestine for various personal or political reasons. Although the details of v. 11 do not seem to fit this view literally ("in every place incense is offered to my name, and a pure offering"), one may also understand them metaphorically, as symbols of the genuine faith of Jews living among non-Jews.

The phrase "for my name is great among the nations, says the LORD of hosts," together with its parallel in v. 14b, "my name is feared among the nations," is of special interest. It is tempting to link it with its opposite, e.g., in Ezek. 36:19-21, where "the house of Israel" is rebuked ("wherever they came, they profaned my holy name," v. 20). In Ezekiel's view the exile of the people of God was interpreted as a disgrace to God's name. But Deutero-Isaiah believes that the dispersion might be a chance to spread the gospel of justice and truth, and Malachi seems to see signs of this happening.

Such openness can also be found in both early and later Judaism despite the narrow position expressed in Deuteronomy, Ezra, and Nehemiah. Of course, these books had their necessary function, as those two great men Ezra and Nehemiah had in building up a new and well-knit community. Yet the Jews never forgot that their God was greater than their own ideas and understanding of him. There are many examples of such a broader and deeper view of God.

From preexilic times, Amos can be quoted as seeing God as the guiding power of all nations, judging all according to one principle: justice (Amos 1 – 2; 9:7). Similarly Isaiah (10:5-6), Jeremiah (25:15ff.), and Ezekiel (chs. 25 – 32) uttered threats and judgments against many nations. This too shows an understanding of Israel as part of the whole family of nations under one and the same God, the God of Israel.

During and after the Exile, two general lines of thought can be distinguished: one emphasizing God's merciful intention to cause the light of his salvation to shine over all nations (Isa. 42:4, 6b; 49:6b; 51:4); the other characterizing the nations as enemies of God whose punishment is imminent and directly related to Israel's salvation (Isa. 24:10-23; 60:10-16; Ezek. 38 – 39; Dan. 7:2 – 12:3). Although the former line of thought is not as well known as the latter, it is certainly the more important: it constitutes a direct link to the life and teaching of Jesus. Isa. 2:2-4 (and Mic. 4:1-3) may be compared with 25:6-8; 55:5; 56:3, 6-8; and, for example, with Matt. 8:5-13 (esp. v. 11; cf. Luke 13:29; Acts 10). The book of Jonah was surely meant as a powerful witness of God's love embracing all people — even Nineveh, the capital of Israel's most hated enemy, Assyria. So Jonah must be understood as a protest against any one-sided claim to "absolute truth" that would reject others. Many stories in the rest of the OT also helped people to remember that the God of Israel was the God of all humankind (see, e.g., Gen. 14:18-20; 20:1-18; Exod. 18:10-12; 2 Kgs. 5; Ps. 22:27-31; 47:7-9). Viewed in this way Mal. 1:11 clearly does not present an extreme or isolated point of view. Nevertheless, it certainly bursts the bounds of a religious ideology that tries to transform God into an easily manageable possession.

. . . or Claims to Christian Absolutism?

Absolutist attitudes of some factions of Judaism are not isolated opinions limited to this religious group; in fact every kind of religious movement has produced attitudes of this sort. The remarkable openness of Jesus is beyond question (Matt. 8:10; see Mark 7:24-30), while Peter and Paul, together with the rest of the apostles, had to learn this through many experiences (see, e.g., Acts 10; 13:46-47; 15:1-29; Gal. 2:7-21). Yet it appears that the pressure of persecutions during the first centuries of the Christian Church, the constant danger to communities and individuals (see, e.g., 1 Pet. 1:6-9; Rev. 2–3), and the fear of being unfaithful to their Lord (see, e.g., Rom. 12:1-2; 1 Pet. 4:12-19; 2 Tim. 4:1-5) have caused Christians to develop distrustful attitudes toward non-Christians. So after Christianity became a "state religion" (under Constantine in A.D. 391) all "pagan cults" were prohibited. Later a theological argument was also produced: "outside the church there is no salvation!" This is surely not what John meant by preaching Jesus as "the way, and the truth, and the life" (14:6).

Tracing the relationship between Christians and non-Christians throughout the centuries and even in our own time is saddening. Frequently this relationship is characterized by an un-Christian arrogance which claims "absolute truths" for itself and forgets that nothing is absolute except God. Recently, however, the situation has changed, mainly due to two developments:

1. The growing self-awareness of non-Western peoples of, among other things, their own cultural heritage and the exploitation exercised by selfish, Western, so-called Christian nations,

who have failed to live up to the demands of Christ: that Christians ought to be peace-loving, selfless, just, and humane.

2. The remarkable "enlightenment" experienced by many members of different religious traditions worldwide who are beginning to see each other less as promoters of competing creeds and more as people who try, according to their individual understanding of what is "true" and "good," to make this world a better place to live in.

Can this be a part of the Kingdom of God? Paradoxically, perhaps, these two developments are the results of the work of missionaries during the past two hundred years. Unfailingly, these missionaries have gained a profound understanding of and respect for the value of non-Western cultural heritages and also of the sincerity of their religious attitudes. Further, they did not remain aloof to the wrongdoings of their fellow Westerners in military, trade, and other activities.

According to Matt. 8:10, Jesus acknowledged the faith of a Roman soldier (see also Matt. 15:21-28). Isa. 7:9b (and 28:16) similarly describe "faith" as a complete commitment to God (see Rom. 9:24-33) and not as the claim to "truth" which has to be believed (see Jas. 2:14-26). Such an understanding can help one to acknowledge the existence of "faith" where we would normally not expect it: outside our own sphere of experience.

This does not, of course, mean that we should abandon what we ourselves have received: God's grace and acceptance, or in biblical terms, his election, covenant, and salvation, through the witnesses in the OT and the NT, particularly in Jesus' self-giving love (see Rom. 11:25-36). People who let themselves be called by God in this manner will know that he who calls them is greater than their own understanding of him. Furthermore, this will determine their commitment to serve and love him (see Luke 10:29-37).

DO NOT GO BACK ON WHAT YOU HAVE VOWED!
(1:12-14)

Although Malachi may have an open-minded standpoint concerning non-Jews, he does not take what his community has received lightly: they must still hear the demands of the Torah concerning sacrifices offered to God on the altar at Jerusalem. These demands are valid and have to be taken very seriously.

13   The priests consider it a "weariness" to do their job properly, i.e., to find out what gifts are being brought to the temple and whether they are proper according to the rules. What is actually offered on the altar is their responsibility. Not checking the quality of the offerings is equal to despising the LORD's altar. This principle has also caused some earnest Christians throughout history to reject certain gifts offered to the Church. It may also explain the remark at Matt. 27:6 about the silver coins which Judas brought back into the temple: "It is not lawful to put them into the treasury, since they are blood money."

Verse 13 contains some slight difficulties. The Hebrew term translated as "sniff" actually means "pant," as in "you make me *pant*," i.e., cause me to be angry, or hot. "Your" in "you bring as *your* offering," in the RSV, is an interpretation which may obscure the fact that this passage speaks of something the priests must do before offering the gifts of the people. This intention is evident in v. 14 where those who first make a vow and then change their mind are cursed. Going back on one's vow in this manner is trying to cheat God!

The last clause brings an interesting variant to v. 11: "my name is feared among the nations." This formulation underlines the statement in v. 11 and confirms its meaning. We have seen in v. 6 that "the fear of the LORD is the beginning of wisdom" (Prov. 9:10). It seems difficult to assume that Mal. 1:14b means anything less than this. To be sure, "fear" is also used with other meanings elsewhere (see, e.g., Zeph. 2:11), but the particular situation of Malachi and his community in this passage has to be considered carefully.

CHAPTER 2

A PROPHETIC INDICTMENT OF THE LEVITICAL PRIESTS (2:1-9)

Introduction (2:1-2)

1-2 The address in 1:6 included the priests. Now they are singled out, so that the following is about their particular duty. Verse 2 once more takes up the theme "to give glory to my name" (1:6-11). The contrast is as striking here as it was in 1:11; the "nations" are presented as examples of those who honor God, while the people of God are criticized for failing to do so. Malachi proceeds to link this honoring or dishonoring of God to the "blessings" the priests expect. "Blessing" and "cursing" are two important themes in Deuteronomy. The message of this book declares that blessing accompanies obedience to Torah as surely as disobedience calls forth the curse (see, e.g., 4:1; 5:1; 6:1-3; and esp. 28:1-68; 30:15-20). In Mal. 2:1-2, however, the writer seems to refer more specifically to Deut. 33:9-11, where we find words concerning Levi, in the so-called Blessings of Moses. Both expressions in v. 2 — "if you do not listen" (see Deut. 6:4; 28:15) and "if you will not lay it to heart" (see Deut. 6:6; 11:18) — are taken from the Shema (i.e., Deut. 6:4-9, which begins with "Hear [Heb. *shemaʿ*], O Israel"). This is the prayer that every pious Jew has recited at least once a day from early times to the present. Malachi did not use these words by accident. They serve to point out the basis for his critique. From Malachi's point of view one fact was beyond doubt for all: life in disobedience to the Torah would be cursed, not blessed. It is a point of view that must be taken seriously in our everyday lives.

Warning (2:3-4)

3 There are two uncertainties here in the Hebrew text. (1) "I will rebuke your offspring" (cf., e.g., the NEB and W. Rudolph, *Maleachi:* "I will cut off your arm"); and (2) "I will put you out of my presence" (cf., e.g., Rudolph, "you will become a curse-word"). The former is the more serious divergence from the RSV, and at least the correction "I will cut off" is preferable to the RSV translation. It certainly makes better sense. The LXX uses a word with the meaning "to take away," and not "to rebuke." The reason for the divergence mentioned above was most probably a spelling mistake in a later copy of the Hebrew text. The threat to the priests must be meant as a serious punishment, like "cut off" or "take away."

The second difficulty, however, is not very serious: according to ancient thinking, a person who is denied the presence of God is cursed, and he himself will become an example of the curse (see, e.g., Deut. 29:24-28; Ps. 44:13-16). A cursed person became an object of scorn and derision — one against whom people would throw dung or excrement in order to express utter contempt (see, e.g., Nah. 3:6). Dung was something very "unclean" in the cultic sense (see, e.g., Exod. 29:14; Deut. 23:12-13).

4 The continuation in v. 4 is difficult. The NEB reads: "Then you will know that I have issued this decree against you: *my covenant with Levi falls to the ground. . . .*" This different text is due to a conjectured correction of one Hebrew word, *lehyot* (RSV "hold"). The RSV renders the Hebrew reliably and expresses a clear intention: the curse (v. 3) is meant to be a warning, reprimand, and exhortation with the aim "that my covenant with Levi may hold." When this passage is seen in the total context of 1:6 – 2:9 such an intention can hardly be doubted.

Exposition (2:5-7)

These verses develop the topic further, in two steps: (a) by presenting an idealized tradition concerning Levi (vv. 5-6); (b) by spelling out what is to be expected of a priest (v. 7).

The Sons of Levi The name "Levi" (v. 4) may cause some confusion. In some books of the OT the "Levites" or "sons of Levi" are the priests. In other writings priests and "Levites" are two clearly different groups of people. Here are some details: the "sons of Levi" were the "Levitical priests" (e.g., Exod. 6:16-20; 32:25-29; Deut. 17:9; 18:1-8; 21:5; 31:9). Aaron, Moses' brother, was a son of Levi and the first Levitical priest. However, the "centralization" of the cult at Jerusalem (see at 1:11) had two consequences: (1) there were now too many priests (see, e.g., Deut. 18:6-8); (2) the priests at Jerusalem decided that none of the others should be allowed to serve at the temple. The official reason given can be found in 2 Kgs. 23:8-9, and also in Ezek. 44:10-13. This was the time at which a distinction between "Levites" and "priests" was made. The Levitical priests at Jerusalem officially remained priests while those from the rest of the country were now "Levites." This subsequently became the rule, as is evident from Exod. 28:1; Num. 3:1-13 (see further, e.g., Num. 8:5ff.; 18:6-7; Ezek. 40:46). According to this rule the "Levites" were the "assistants" of Aaron and his sons. Later still, another change came about, which was due to a power struggle within the priests' group at Jerusalem. Zadok, a priest during David's time, being a "local," became the legal head of the priests at Jerusalem (see, e.g., Ezek. 44:15; 2 Sam. 15:24; 1 Kgs. 1; Ezra 7:2). Zadok thus replaced Abiathar, who was originally the only priest of David (1 Sam. 22:20; 23:9; etc.). Abiathar's downfall appears to have occurred when he sided with Adonijah, the rival of Solomon (1 Kgs. 1:7, 25, 42; 2:26-27).

The Covenant with Levi This formulation seems to refer to Deut. 33:9 and intends to point back to the very beginnings of priesthood in Israel. In fact, however, nothing is known of such a "covenant." Deut. 33:9 actually speaks about the covenant of Yahweh with Israel, and not of a separate covenant with the sons of Levi. Perhaps Mal. 2:4-6 reveals a misunderstanding based on Deut. 33. However, the account in Exod. 32:26-29 comes close to establishing such a distinction for the sons of Levi: they earn great praise from Moses: "Today you have ordained yourselves for the service of the LORD" (v. 29).

The Duty of the Priests One of the reasons for assuming that Mal. 2:6-7 is based on Deut. 33:8-11 is the presence of references to the Torah in both of them. Both also regard the teaching of the Torah to the people as the most important duty of the priests. This responsibility is assigned to Aaron and his sons in Lev. 10:11. In Deuteronomy we find several examples of what this means in practice, e.g., advising the future king (17:9, 18), settling disputes (21:5), deciding who is a leper (24:8), and pronouncing the warnings of the Torah (27:14). In Hag. 2:11-13 a priest is asked to advise on a question of "clean and unclean" (see, e.g., Lev. 10:10). In the account of Ezra's bringing of the Torah to the community at Jerusalem, the "Levites" had the task of teaching the people (Neh. 8:9). Apparently this was what remained of their original duty as priests. From the details in Deuteronomy and Neh. 8:9, we can more fully understand why the duty of the priests was so important: they had to teach the people to do the right things in everyday life, on the basis of the Torah. This Torah was the comprehensive guide in all matters of the cultic and secular life of the people. K. Elliger (*Maleachi*, ATD, 189) assumes that in Malachi the distinction between "priests" and "Levites" is still maintained. In the light of Ezek. 44:10-14 this is unlikely. The common origin of the Levites and priests is not questioned anywhere and as such is also the basis for Malachi's argument in 2:1ff.

Indictment and Punishment (2:8-9)

8   The charge leveled at the priests is laid down very clearly in three points: (1) "you have turned aside from the way"; (2) "you have caused many to stumble"; and (3) "you have corrupted the covenant." Note the similar charge in Hos. 4:4-6, which also accuses the priests of unfaithfulness to the Torah. Ezek. 44:10-14 specifies the charges against the Levites, explaining why they cannot be priests anymore: "going astray from me," "becoming a stumbling block" (cf. R. Abba, "Priests and Levites," *IDB*, 3:885).

9   When pronouncing the punishment, Malachi again mentions his reasons. He stresses these important points: "you have not kept my ways," and "[you] have shown partiality in your instruction." This clarifies further the charge concerning the "instruction." To "show partiality" means "to do injustice in judgment" — in favor of the "poor" or the "great" (Lev. 19:15). This is not the way of God, "who is not partial and takes no bribe" (Deut. 10:17). In this whole section it should be noted that "instruction" is the translation of *torah* (RSV mg notes the alternative rendering, "law"). The priestly "torah" mentioned here is not necessarily in all details identical to the "Torah" of Ezra (7:6, 10). Ezra's Torah appears to have been a compilation of instructions which in content were very similar to a large portion of the books Exodus through Deuteronomy. But the "priests' torah" referred to here may indicate only part of that material. Hence Malachi distinguishes between the priestly "instruction" and "the way" of God (vv. 8-9). This charge is very serious when one considers the position of the Torah in the life of the community, and the responsibility of the priests as teachers and counselors of the people.

Faithlessness to God and Fellow Human Beings
(2:10-12)

This section links 2:1-9 with 2:13-16: the complaint about "faithlessness" results from the wrong or insufficient instruction given by the priests. At the same time it anticipates the topic of divorce.

10 Here there is a definite change of style. The "messenger" is now speaking directly to his countrymen, even including his own person — "have we not all one father?" (i.e., God, our creator). This cry is a plea for unity and for loyalty to the traditions of the fathers.

11 Taking these traditions seriously would mean being loyal to one another and to one's religion. Here Malachi shows the religious implication of a matter which might otherwise have been dismissed as being of no great consequence: marriage with non-Jewish women. The stern character of vv. 11-12 has caused some commentators to assume that these verses, or at least some of them, were added at a later date. Indeed, they do not compare well with 1:11! The tone is very much like that of Ezra 9–10 and Neh. 13:23ff. But from another point of view this reprimand has considerable actuality for all persons belonging to groups with strong religious and moral principles.

12 Malachi even adds a curse, denying such a person any fellowship: support in court ("witness"), companionship ("answer"), or even help in cultic matters (the RSV is preferable to the NEB). However, the charge and the curse can only be understood properly if one tries to appreciate the situation of the postexilic community: it had to live under great pressure from its non-Israelite neighbors. Some national and religious minorities in many parts of the world today understand what the pressure of the large society means for the small community.

The indications are that both the common people and at least some of their spiritual and political leaders did not take the charge of v. 11 very seriously: "Judah has been faithless . . . has profaned the sanctuary of the LORD." "Sanctuary," in Hebrew, *qodesh*, the "holy" (thing, place, etc.), has a broad meaning. It includes all that belongs to God and has been entrusted to the people, and especially to the priests. Here the term "profaned" is used together with the word "holy," indicating a charge usually leveled against priests alone (see, e.g, Lev. 19:8; 22:15; Ezek. 22:26; Zeph.

3:4). In this instance the charge is being leveled at the *people* called Judah, together with the charge of having been "faithless." Similar charges are made in Hos. 5:7; 6:7 (Israel); Jer. 3:8, 11, 20; 5:11.

The charge made here explains both Malachi's anger and his excitement: that Judah "has married the daughter of a foreign god" indicates not a mere negligible social affair, but a repetition of what had previously brought about the downfall of Judah. The "daughter of a foreign god" is not just any foreigner, but one who leads Judah astray to "serve foreign gods" (see, e.g., Deut. 13:6-11; 31:16), resulting in her punishment (Jer. 5:19; 8:19; Deut. 31:16-19; 2 Kgs. 17:7ff.). What had once more been entrusted to the renewed community — the land of their fathers, the people, and the revived sanctuary (which had been dedicated only in 515 B.C.) — was again being profaned! This "messenger" of ours could hardly believe that all that had happened to Israel in the past had been forgotten, for example, the great national disaster in 587 B.C., its cruel effect on the people, its political and religious consequences. Those who had returned from the Exile definitely saw these events of the past as God's punishment for the faithlessness of their fathers so that they experienced the new opportunities in Judah and at Jerusalem as God's grace (Zech. 1:1-6).

LET NONE BE UNFAITHFUL TO THE WIFE OF HIS YOUTH (2:13-16)

13 "And this again you do," actually, "this is the second thing you do," thus introducing the second charge in this question of "marriage." The second differs from the first in that it deals with the problem of divorce. In other respects it is still linked to the first by the use of terms like "faithless," "covenant," and "offering" (vv. 10, 12). The description in v. 13 reminds one of the language of Amos 5:22 (see Isa. 26:16), where the people "seek" God (see Hos. 6:1-3) and yet are distressed because God refuses to accept their offerings and prayers (Isa. 1:12-15; cf. Jer. 2:27b). In ancient times there were many methods by which people thought they could recognize whether an offering had been accepted (see, e.g., 1 Sam. 14:36-42; Ps. 5:3), although we do not know very much about them. Such a seeking of God had a variety of causes, for example, a defeat (Judg. 20:26-28), or a bad harvest (Hag. 1:5-6, 9-10; 2:16-17). These causes were usually seen as the result of the people's wrongdoings (Deut. 28:25ff.; Amos 4:6-12).

14   The critical response of the people addressed by the "messenger" is quite defiant: "Why does he not?" The reply of the "messenger" mentions the "covenant" twice. This seems to have been a kind of wedding ceremony, including the swearing of an oath. But in the OT and other early Jewish traditions we do not find such "covenants." Ruth 4:9-12 reflects a very simple social contract, concluded in the gate, with blessings pronounced. This contract was legally binding but could be dissolved as provided for in Deut. 24:1-4. The position of the wife as "companion" is comparable to that in Gen. 2:18, 20, translated in the RSV as "helper," but in the NEB more correctly as "partner" (as proposed by M. Buber, *Die fünf Bücher der Weisung*). The reply emphasizes this positive relationship which accords with God's will as described in the Torah. The reason for their distress is their "faithlessness," the destruction of this good relationship. The "messenger" introduces the term "divorce" only in v. 16, but the matter is already fully expressed at this point. Here the style also changes to the singular, perhaps to make this particular charge more personal and direct.

15   In spite of what can be said about the positive relationship between a man and his wife, the fact remains that "divorce" was made relatively easy for the husband (Deut. 24:1; Matt. 5:31-32). This view must be seen in the total context of ancient Near Eastern culture. The reason for this new and much stricter approach in Mal. 2:14-16 must be sought in the theological and moral developments which had taken place during the Exile in Babylon. These ideas were brought back to Jerusalem and Judah by the returnees, after 538 B.C. (see Isa. 56).

The question remains: was it in fact the issue of "divorce" alone which made the "messenger" speak up in this manner when replying to the distressed people with whom he was arguing? Verse 15a consists of two questions, the first of which is difficult to translate (see, e.g., the RSV mg and NEB mg). "Has not the one God made" may also be translated as "He has not made one (only)." This translation then points to the creation narrative in Gen. 2:18, 21-22. The following two words (RSV mg "remnant" and "spirit") are probably wrongly vocalized in Hebrew (see W. Rudolph, *Maleachi*, 270) and actually mean "flesh" and "completion" (or "expansion"). This can be formulated, for greater clarity, as "he has not made (or created) one only, but has completed him by adding another human being." This reflects Gen. 2:23-24. Hence, this first sentence is not a question but a statement.

The question which follows also begins with "One." In this case, "One" will refer to God, as in the Shema (Deut. 6:4). The answer to this, "godly offspring," can hardly mean anything other than "purely Jewish" (see Ezra 9:2, "holy race"). This brings us back to the problem of the "daughter of a foreign god." Even if we translate "descendants according to the will of God" (W. Rudolph, *Maleachi*, 270) it still means the same when read in the context of Malachi's community and in the light of Ezra 9 – 10 and Neh. 13. This conclusion has often been rejected, but it seems wrong to isolate Malachi from his contemporary community in this one respect while acknowledging that they shared almost everything else. The warnings at the end of v. 15 (and 16) add further weight to this conclusion.

When considering this issue also in the light of 1:11 and what has been seen there as one possible implication, another question might arise. On the one hand, Malachi appears to be open to God's working outside Israelite tradition; on the other hand, he strictly forbids marriage with persons outside this tradition. K. Elliger (*Maleachi*, ATD, 189, 200, 204) considers this tension as sufficient evidence that both verses cannot have been part of Malachi's original words. In fact, however, this is no contradiction. In traditional societies (not only Jewish) the parents decide who their children are going to marry. The chosen partner is, of course, one of their own religious and national group. Hence the prohibition of divorce has at least two functions: it provides for the stability of the traditional society, and it ensures the continuity of traditional religious practice. To acknowledge God's working outside one's own tradition and experience does not at all mean that one could or should abandon one's tradition (see at 1:11). For the early Jewish community both in Babylon and in Judea, the supreme concern was to live according to God's will in order to remain in God's newly granted favor: to be blessed and have a future.

From the above we may understand furthermore that Malachi is not simply teaching faithfulness within marriage. His own theological concern and that of many biblical witnesses is the relationship between God and his people. The term "covenant" (v. 14) brings to mind the covenantal relationship which God had established with Israel (Exod. 24:1-11). Hosea translated this into the picture of the relationship of husband and wife (chs. 1 – 3). In addition, Deutero-Isaiah also reminded the exiled people that God had not broken off this relationship (Isa. 50:1). With this in mind, the demand "So take heed to yourselves, and let none be faithless to the wife of his youth" (v. 15b) carries much greater weight than a mere moral exhortation. It is a warning not to rebel against the covenant God has made with his people. With respect to the modern Christian situation we may see the English "covenant" (noun and verb) in the marriage ceremony as an echo of the covenant of God in the OT, "you will be my people and I will be your God."

16 It should not be denied, however, that the period of the Exile gave rise to many new ideas and developments in theological and moral thought. The very statement "for I hate divorce" points to such a new understanding. It is the only such statement in the OT and Jewish literature (but see Matt. 5:31-32). Many strict rules were actually introduced by the Hasidic movement, which began in the exilic community and gave rise to the Pharisaic and Essene groups. One of the marks of these was a harsh rigorism in all religious and moral matters linked to the lifestyle of true Jews (M. Hengel, *Judaism and Hellenism*, 1:175ff.). Such rigorism came into existence as a result of an eagerness to live in accordance with the Torah in order to protect the people of God from any new downfall. The last clause, "covering one's garment with violence," may be compared with similar expressions in Ps. 73:6 and Isa. 59:6. It describes "divorce" as "wickedness," i.e., as something done by those who displease God. The teaching in Matt. 5:31-32 probably goes back to similar roots. Neither Mal. 2:13-16 nor Matt. 5:31-32 is in fact directly concerned with the status of women in society. But both have the common objective of enforcing stricter moral rules guarding against adultery, which, according to the Torah, is not just a woman's crime but also a man's. In this, the OT, Judaism, and the NT reveal a far higher regard for women than the literature of any of the neighboring nations at that time.

RIGHT AND WRONG: CONFUSING MORAL VALUES (2:17)

This verse deals with one independent topic: that of justice in the community. The passage that follows it, 3:1-5, addresses the same topic, but from the very different perspective of hope and promise. "Justice" is a demand of the Torah, and its proper administration depends on the faithful teaching of the Torah. In this respect, the central importance of 2:1-9 is again evident.

The beginning of v. 17, "You have wearied the LORD with your words," should be read in the light of 2:7-9 (see Jer. 23:21-22) but with special application to the administration of justice. Many passages in the Torah condemn injustice, especially when it takes the form of partiality (see, e.g., Exod. 23:7-8; Lev. 19:15; Deut. 1:17; 16:19). Particularly vocal in this respect were the prophets (Amos 2:6-7; 5:7, 12; Isa. 5:20, 23). Isaiah made the special point of condemning those who tried to make others believe that there was no straightforward guideline for distinguishing between good and evil. The subject of injustice in the administration of the law is also mentioned in the Wisdom literature (see, e.g., Prov. 17:15; 18:5; 24:23-24). The "law" (Torah) of the Jewish community was not "secular" as opposed to some kind of "spiritual" law. Although, in our day, we might resort to this kind of classification, such a distinction is unknown to the Torah. The Torah addresses all aspects of life. The same Torah handled both secular and spiritual aspects, and God was the giver as well as the guardian of this Torah. The question "Where is the God of justice?" may then be understood in two ways: (1) as a cynical question (see, e.g., Isa. 5:19; 29:15; Jer. 17:15), or (2) as an honestly troubled one. The answer to the latter would then be given in 3:1-5.

Almost all the passages mentioned above deal with "partiality" in one way or another (cf. 2:9b). These passages, however, do not refer to complicated legal matters. Instead, they deal with issues relating to individuals or groups who are treated unjustly because of their sex, their position in society, or their financial means. One can easily relate these examples of injustice to situations in our own world today. Such injustices, especially partiality toward powerful interest groups in the realms of the economy and of industry, that harm the weaker strata of society, and in particular in the so-called developing countries, are only too common. People often try to explain these facts away, but a society which allows, condones, and even promotes such partiality for its own benefit is unjust. K. Elliger (*Maleachi*, ATD, 205-206) stresses the eschatological dimension of 2:17 and 3:1-5. The coming of God to his people and to his temple would be strictly speaking an eschatological event, because this would bring about all that the still oppressed Jewish community was hoping for, in the elimination of injustice.

CHAPTER 3

THE GOD OF JUSTICE IS COMING (3:1-5)

The question "Where is the God of justice?" (2:17) expresses
more than just a cynical rejection of faith in such a God. It may
well be merely the anxious sigh of a faith that is troubled by
doubt and by unending experiences of injustice. Prophets have
often used the literary styles of visions, auditions, or other reve-
lations to describe their deepest understanding and conviction
(see, e.g., Amos 7 – 9; Isa. 6; Jer. 1). In this instance very obviously the "messenger" has two special reasons to express himself in a similar manner: (1) he feels compelled to state on what
authority he dares to criticize so severely what the priests are
doing, or are failing to do; (2) the question raised by the sufferers
(2:17, last clause) urges him to find words of comfort for those
who cannot see an end to the injustice they are being forced to
bear. Accordingly this section brings three points to light: (1) it
introduces an explanation of the "messenger's" role in God's plans
(vv. 1-2); (2) it promises the purification of the "sons of Levi" so
that the people's offerings will once more become acceptable to
the LORD (vv. 3-4); (3) furthermore, it promises that justice will
be restored in accordance with the demands of the Torah (v. 5).
With these positive points, then, Malachi takes up the questions
arising from his messages in 1:6 – 2:17.

The Messenger of the LORD (3:1-3)

1 Considering this verse in the prevailing context, particularly
in the light of the preceding sections, the "messenger's" identity
should not be in doubt at this stage. This word, styled as a direct
speech of Yahweh, describes the messenger as "sent by Yahweh."
His task is to "prepare the way" for Yahweh's coming. This an-
nouncement is intended by the editor of the book to be a response
to the question asked in 2:17: "Where is the God of justice?"
Beside Malachi, Deutero-Isaiah (40:3), Matthew (3:3; 11:10),
and the other Gospels also take up this call to "prepare the way

100

of the LORD." On his part, Deutero-Isaiah calls on the exiled people of God to make themselves ready for God's coming (40:9-11; see 62:11) so that he may guide them back to their place. He proclaims the message of salvation: God will again accept his people, forgive and heal them, and renew their community.

On the other hand, the Gospel passages refer in this manner to John the Baptist as the one who is seen as the forerunner and preparer "of the way of the Lord" (i.e., Jesus). So, formally, the "coming of the Lord" is then understood as being the public ministry of Jesus. Theologically, however, it was taken to be God's own coming: he was seen to be with Jesus, in his life, work, death, and finally in his resurrection from the dead (Luke 2:40, 52; 24:19, 34; John 3:2; 7:31; 9:33; Rom. 1:4).

The above passages from Deutero-Isaiah and the Gospels can not guide our understanding of Mal. 3:1. But Deutero-Isaiah may nevertheless suggest to us the direction of the original intention of Mal. 3: the coming of the LORD means "salvation." For Malachi, however, this salvation does not come without judgment: "the LORD . . . will suddenly come." Judgment comes because people ignore God's warnings (Isa. 48:3-5; Ps. 78:5-8). The prophets' stern messages are intended to stop people from doing evil, so that they will not be judged. On the other hand, once judgment has been suffered, salvation is on the way (Isa. 40:1-2).

The second sentence, "the messenger of the covenant in whom you delight," repeats the first one but suggests that God himself is his own "messenger," in that it was God who originally gave the covenant. However, it is possible that Moses, the traditional mediator of the covenant, may be meant here (see Mark 9:4; John 1:17). The whole of Malachi is concerned with God's covenant, the sole chance for the people's renewal. The Torah is the framework of such renewal, so both belong together. But "messenger," Heb. *mal'ak*, can also be translated as "angel." This suggests that the "angel of the covenant" is alluding to the Exodus narrative, especially Exod. 23:20-21, "hearken to his voice" (see Freedman and Willoughby, *"mal'ak," TWAT*, 4:898). The point here, of course, is not to encourage a "new exodus" but rather to foster obedience to the Torah. It is not very clear, however, exactly what Malachi may have meant with this unique title, "messenger/angel of the covenant." The relative clause, "in whom you delight," has a possible cynical meaning (see v. 2 and Joel 2:1; Amos 5:18). Nevertheless, it has to be considered that "angel" appears essentially to be a statement of Yahweh's presence with people for whom he cares, or sometimes as confronting those who rebel against him (see, e.g., Gen. 16:7-14; 21:17; Num. 22:22-30; and Freedman and Willoughby, *"mal'ak," TWAT*, 4:898, 901).

The word "suddenly" suggests that the coming of God was expected in the manner of "the day of the LORD" known in Israel's tradition since Amos (see, e.g., 5:18, 20; Isa. 13:6; Joel 1:15; Obad. 15). NT writers take up the idea of the "sudden" coming of the judgment day (Matt. 24:27, 36-44, et al.; 1 Thess. 5:2-3; 2 Pet. 3:10; Rev. 3:3; 16:15). Their descriptions are strongly influenced by apocalyptic ideas of "the end of the world." They add to these descriptions that of the salvation of the faithful by the Lord himself (1 Thess. 4:16-17).

2-3 In Malachi, however, the day of the LORD is not thought of as a time of total destruction, but rather as a time of purification (as in Isa. 1:24-26). The symbols of "refining" are often used, but with varying expectations (see, e.g., Isa. 48:10; Jer. 6:29-30; Zech. 13:9). Most of the passages which deal with this subject speak of the people in general as needing to be refined (except Isa. 1:25-26), but here the objects of purification are "the sons of Levi."

God Shall Rule (3:4-5)

4 This verse obviously refers back to 1:6ff., in particular to the people's and the priests' insincere attitude toward God in presenting their gifts. As a result these gifts were not "pleasing" to God. However, Mal. 3:4 goes much further than the critique ". . . will be pleasing to the LORD as in the days of old and as in former years." On the "day of his coming," God will "refine" and "purify." In other words, on that day the people, the priests, and what they do will be renewed (cf. Jer. 31:31-34). This day of salvation is compared with an ideal time "in the days of old." This does not necessarily mean that those "days of old" were actually "ideal" (see, e.g., Deut. 1:26-45), but rather that they were remembered as a time when God acted in a special manner by giving Israel the covenant and the Torah. This is also true of Solomon (see, e.g., 1 Kgs. 3:3, 10-11; and compare it with 11:1-11). Some traditions have preserved the memory of an ideal time in the past (Hos. 2:15b; Isa. 1:26; Jer. 2:2-3), which will occur again in the future when God intervenes once more in Israel's history.

5 The time of salvation will bring God's rule. Trito-Isaiah (65:17ff.) describes it as "I create new heavens and a new earth." The rule of God will also restore the rights of the people and do

away with injustice (Isa. 65:21, 22a; 32:16-18, going back, most
probably to 1:26b, 27). In a similar fashion Mal. 3:5 describes
how God will establish justice in this coming time. It is worth
noting which details are mentioned: magic (Exod. 20:7; 22:18),
adultery (Exod. 20:14), perjury (Exod. 20:16), and oppression of
defenseless persons (Deut. 5:14-15; see Exod. 22:21-22; Deut.
24:14-15). All of these are found in the Torah. This reminds the
reader that God's rule is in accordance with his "instruction,"
accomplishing what the priests and the people had refused to do.
It is not difficult to draw parallels to Christian expectations of
the Kingdom of God, which according to Jesus will be a kingdom
of justice (see, e.g., Matt. 25:31ff.).

Both Mal. 3:5 and Matt. 25:31ff. use the dramatic description
of the "judgment day," but the details of each are very different.
Whereas in Mal. 3:5 this judgment is directed at obvious evildoers and comes together with the saving renewal, Matt. 25:31ff.
is about the judgment of all people, separating the evil from the
good. Hence the implications of both descriptions are also very
different. In Mal. 3:5 the judgment against those "who do not
fear" God is a saving, renewing action in the Jewish community.
But Matt. 25:31ff. sees humanity divided into two groups at the
end of time. Some are invited, "Come, O blessed of my Father,
inherit the kingdom prepared for you" (v. 34); and the others are
told, "Depart from me, you cursed, into the eternal fire" (v. 41).
For Malachi, however, as we have said, this renewal and judgment
describe the people of God in the renewed and healed relationship
of the covenant with God (see, e.g., Jer. 31:31-34; Isa. 61:10-11).

PUT THE LORD TO THE TEST! (3:6-12)

The structure of this section is complicated: v. 6, introduction;
v. 7a, b, accusation and demand (subject Yahweh); v. 7c, (8a),
question (subject people); v. 8b, accusation (subject Yahweh);
v. 8c, question (subject people); vv. 8d, 9, accusation (subject
Yahweh); vv. 10-12, request and promise (subject Yahweh).

6 The discussion is introduced by a twofold statement which is
formulated as spoken by Yahweh: v. 6a, "For I the LORD do not
change!"; v. 6b, "therefore you, O sons of Jacob, are not consumed." On the surface, both statements are in harmony and
agree well with the conclusion of the preceding section (v. 5),
suggesting that God will not forsake his people (cf. Hos. 11:8-9;
Isa. 40:27-28). These statements introduce a new section, how-

ever, so the continuation in v. 7 does not agree with an interpretation such as the RSV's, "From the days of your fathers you have turned aside." The problem lies with the words "not consumed." The word "consumed" itself is not in doubt (cf. Isa. 1:28; 29:20). But it is possible that the word "not" is a later addition and that the original text was "therefore . . . you are consumed." Such later changes are known to have been made in other passages (see, e.g., Jer. 4:27; 5:10, 18; 46:28) and were intended to comfort the people. Another possibility would be to read a contrasting word like "but" instead of "therefore" (RSV) and explain this contrast as the paradox of God's love and patience with his people (cf. Isa. 43:18-28).

7 Both the accusation and the demand are often found in several books of earlier prophets, especially in Jeremiah (2:5-8; 7:25-26; see also 3:12, 14, 22; 4:1). The sentence "Return to me, and I will return to you," together with v. 12a, "Then all nations will call you blessed," is a bracket which holds this section together. Both belong to the so-called covenant tradition which recalls the mutual relationship between Yahweh and the people (see, e.g., Exod. 19:5; Jer. 11:4). This is the source of real blessing (Deut. 7:6-16; 26:16-19; Jer. 4:2; 7:6-7).

Can Human Beings Cheat God?

The statement in v. 7, "But you say . . . ," implies a serious accusation, because it alludes to the claim in Deuteronomy, "Yet you . . . rebelled" (see Deut. 1:26, 43; 2 Kgs. 17:14). Jer. 7:26 expresses plainly what this means: "yet they did not listen to me . . . but stiffened their neck," "they refused to repent" (5:3). This has to do, of course, with the "return" to God (Deut. 4:30; 30:2; Jer. 3:7; 4:1). The "messenger" has repeatedly criticized the lack of such a return, which comes about only when living in accordance with the demands of the Torah (Mal. 1:6-7, 12-13; 2:8-9: cf. Matt. 5:19-20). Consequently he now underscores that fact in order to emphasize the people's unwillingness to return.

8 The first and second sentences could be understood as a question and its answer. Both of them, however, introduce the subject, so both must be read as words spoken by the "messenger" on God's behalf. The third sentence again quotes the critical and doubting response of the people, and the last sentence finally gives the answer: the people refuse to give to the Levites and priests what is due to them, i.e., the required contributions to the temple which are the income of the Levites and priests (see below).

The Hebrew verb qb^c, "to rob," is used three times in this verse. The address "sons of Jacob" in v. 6 strongly suggests a connection between "Jacob," from the Hebrew root ^cqb (meaning "heel," "end," "behind," and also "to cheat") and the verb "to rob." This is further supported by the LXX, which translates by "to cheat" (see JB). The metathesis of the letters ^cqb and qb^c may have happened unintentionally. If so this means that the text may have originally read: "Will man *cheat* God. . . ." Incidentally, only one other passage apart from Mal. 3:8, 9 has the word qb^c, "rob" — Prov. 22:23. There, this meaning fits the context well.

The charge of "cheating God" thus takes up the popular etymology of the patriarch Jacob's name in Gen. 25:26; 27:36; Hos. 12:7 (here "Ephraim" is another name for "Jacob"). It should be noted, however, that this is not the correct explanation of the name "Jacob." In fact "Jacob" is a popular Northwest Semitic name meaning "He (i.e., God) protects." It is derived from another root ^cqb, with the meaning "to protect." In Malachi's time the first meaning was applied. Hence, assuming the metathesis ($qb^c \rightarrow {}^cqb$), the address "O sons of Jacob" already implies the accusation of "cheating" God (v. 6b).

The people are accused of cheating when paying their dues to the temple. These dues consist of the "tithes" (i.e., the tenth part of the harvested goods) and of "contributions." Tithing was an ancient institution of unknown origin and of varying applications at different times (see, e.g., Deut. 14:22-29). By Malachi's time the income obtained by tithing was destined for the Levites (cf. Num. 18:21-26; Neh. 13:10, 12). The term "contribution" or "offering" (RSV) may include tithes (see Num. 18:24). In Malachi and in Neh. 13:5, however, it indicates a special and voluntary contribution for the priests and the temple.

Return to God So He Will Return to You (2:9-12)

9 Failing to obey the commands of the Torah brings a curse on the people. Hag. 1:4-6, 10-11, and 2:16-17 illustrate this threat (cf. Exod. 22:29-30; 23:15b, 19a). The "messenger" spoke of an actual situation in his day that he interpreted as living under a "curse." Other passages offer many examples of what such curses may have been like, e.g., a drought (Amos 4:6-8), locusts (4:9b), plant or human disease (4:9-10), or military defeat (4:11).

10-11 On the other hand, obeying the commands of the Torah and giving God what belongs to him will result in a blessing. This general theme of curse/blessing resulting from disobeying/obeying is a topic of Deut. 28 (see also Lev. 26:3ff.). Mal. 3:10-11 put into simple words a fundamental truth about relationships in general. In human society this principle cannot be ignored: if people wish to live in harmony, there must be this interaction of "give and take." In religious matters, however, people often assume that it is quite "natural" to expect God's blessing. In return they promise to keep from evil. For them this means they should not commit any obviously bad crimes like murder, stealing, or adultery. In fact, this may have been the situation in Malachi's community. This is also what Jesus criticizes in the Sermon on the Mount (Matt. 5—7), where he singles out lack of concern, of generosity, and of courage (cf. 5:20, 22-24, 28, 37, 42, 46-47; 6:2-4, 14-15, 21, 24, 33; 7:2, 20). In other words, the relationship which God grants to his people demands full commitment of body and soul, including their material possessions. A rather frightening example of this is the account of the deaths of Ananias and Sapphira, who tried to cheat God (Acts 5:1-11).

12 This verse alludes to the ancient promise of Gen. 12:3, which has many repetitions and variations (see, e.g., Gen. 18:18; 22:18; Jer. 4:2). In contrast to that promise, Mal. 3:12 has "all nations will call you *blessed.*" The important point is that this "blessing" which so much impresses the nations will be the completion of God's act of renewing his people. Hence they "will be a land of delight" (cf. Zeph. 3:17). Malachi speaks here in the language of the Deuteronomists by linking this promise to the condition in v. 10: "Bring the full tithes . . . and thereby put me to the test" (see also Jer. 17:24-26; 22:4; cf. Deut. 28:1ff.). On the other hand, Trito-Isaiah promises this new status as the gift of God's compassion with his people (Isa. 61:9; 62:2-5). The words "will call you *blessed*" can also be rendered "will *congratulate* you." The same expression is used in Ps. 1:1 and Matt. 5:3 (the Greek equivalent). Psalms, Proverbs, and similar books use this word frequently. Hence the promise in v. 12 may be interpreted as a reformulation of the ancient promise (cf. Deut. 33:29; Zech. 8:13). The reasons for "congratulating" may be God's help (Ps. 41:2), his gifts (Gen. 30:13, RSV "happy"), or the wisdom he grants (Prov. 3:18). The difference from the earlier promise is a new outlook on life, on material and particularly on spiritual possessions (see, e.g., Ps. 2:12; 34:8 — "refuge"; 32:1-2 — "forgiveness"; 40:4 — "faith"; 94:12 — "knowledge of God's instruction").

The eight Beatitudes in Matt. 5 are another example of the same idea. They are, of course, a fruit of the same tree of Jewish

spirituality. Blessings and woe-words as literary types are known
from Deut. 27 and 28, and especially from Psalms and Proverbs.
There is an ongoing development of these types in the Wisdom
literature. Sir. 25:7-11 praises those who are happy. Later apocalyptic writings overflow with woe-words (e.g., the so-called Ethi-
opian or 1 Enoch 94–104), but there are also examples which
compare better with the Beatitudes (1 Enoch 58:2; 99:10; 104:4;
105:2). The woe-word type is also represented in Matthew
(23:13-30; cf. Luke 6:20-26, where some are used in combination).

The solemn concluding phrase, "says the LORD of hosts,"
underlines the importance of this promise of blessedness. This
title is used frequently in Malachi, twenty-three times to be exact!
Details concerning its very ancient origin are uncertain. On the
one hand, from some passages in 1 and 2 Samuel it appears that
this title may have been linked to the ark of the covenant, especially at Shiloh (see, e.g., 1 Sam. 1:3, 11; 4:3-4), but also elsewhere (2 Sam. 6:2, 18). 1 Sam. 17:45 may suggest that "hosts"
means the "armies of Israel." On the other hand, in Exod. 7:4
and 12:51 it means all the people whom God brought up from
Egypt. The prophets occasionally employed this title (see, e.g.,
1 Sam. 15:2; Jer. 15:16; 19:11, 15; 23:15-16; 25:8, 27-29, 32; Hos.
12:5; Amos 3:13; 5:14-16; 6:14; Zeph. 2:9), but no definite pattern
of its usage can be determined, apart from its solemn emphasis
of greatness and power.

GOD'S DAY OF JUDGMENT IS COMING (3:13-18)

Malachi's last topic is again introduced by a reprimand and a
defensive reply expressing surprise: "How have we spoken against
thee?" The structure of this section is somewhat uneven: vv. 13-15
comprise a statement, a question, and an answer; v. 16a may be
reporting the direct result of the foregoing exchange; v. 16b then
reports God's reaction and what happened in heaven; vv. 17-18
add a promise; 4:1 is a threat; and vv. 2-3 bring a prediction.

13 "Stout" (RSV) has the meaning of "stubborn." It is close to
2:17, "You have wearied the LORD with your words," and to
Exod. 7:13, 22; 8:15; and 9:35, where the expression is "to harden
the heart." The question in self-defense that follows confirms this
meaning. Like the other instances quoted in Malachi, this one
expresses the stubborn unwillingness of Levites, priests, and people to accept the guidance of the Torah.

14-15 However, while 2:17-18 may be regarded as a deliberate inversion of moral values, the same cannot be claimed here. This outpouring of an almost nihilistic view of the world is not a deliberate act, but rather a spontaneous expression. It points out the crisis of traditional faith and moral standards. In this respect it comes close to passages in Job (see, e.g., 10:3; 21:7-14: cf. the traditional standards as described by Bildad in 18:3-21). A comparable struggle with moral uncertainty is also found in Ecclesiastes (see, e.g., 2:12-17; 3:16ff.; 4:1ff.). In these two books (Job and Ecclesiastes) the struggle is evidently between two types of religious and moral conviction. In Proverbs and many Psalms this struggle is no longer so obvious because of the strict moral standards which were then applied and adhered to.

Verses 14 and 15 may thus well reflect actual social and religious conditions, and conflicts between rival viewpoints in that postexilic Jewish community to which Malachi also belonged. In Job and in Ecclesiastes, the view prevails that in the end, despite all uncertainties and frustrations, putting one's fate into God's hands and accepting whatever he gives is the only answer to be considered. The terms and formulations in both verses inform us what "to serve God" seems to have meant, at least to one section of the community: "keeping his charge" (see, e.g., Deut. 11:1; Josh. 22:3); "walking as in mourning" (see, e.g., Isa. 58:3); "to be blameless" (see, e.g., Ps. 19:13; 119:51, 69, etc.). This seems to have been the kind of attitude and outward piety which Jesus is said to have referred to in Matt. 6:1-18. The most striking parallels to Mal. 3:14 are Matt. 6:1 and 16 (see also Matt. 23:1-12). However, it would be wrong to single out any group at any time because such formal, pedantic, and joyless rigorism exists everywhere (see, e.g., 1 Sam. 16:7; Mark 14:3-9).

16 Putting one's fate into God's hands as the only solution to the problem is also the answer Malachi offered. But here the evidence of divine reward (which is absent in Job and Ecclesiastes) is known and accepted, in contrast to the earlier complaint (vv. 14-15; cf. Job 21). Verse 16 comprises two scenes, one in the community and one outside the human sphere: "Those who feared the LORD . . . ; the LORD heeded . . . a book of remembrance was written before him." This expresses the attitude of faith which is "the conviction of things not seen" (Heb. 11:1; John 20:29). Yet this description cannot fail to make an impression on the reader as a desperate decision to be on God's side and to cherish the values promoted by the Torah. For a morally oriented person it is unthinkable that those values should not be right. "Those who feared the LORD" are certainly not just people who try "to serve God" (v. 14) in the rigid fashion described above. Much rather they are "the meek" who "shall obtain fresh joy in the LORD, and the poor among men shall exult in the Holy One of Israel" (Isa. 29:19, but see vv. 17-21).

"Book of remembrance" means: God will not fail to remember those who are faithful to him (Exod. 32:32-33; Ps. 69:28; Isa. 4:3; Dan. 12:1; Rev. 20:12). They are witnesses to his love and care as they put their fate into his hands and remain determined to do his will. Of course this had always been the faith and the hope of Israel—but with the expectation that God's saving act on behalf of his faithful would happen within their own lifetime. This verse, however, suggests that the fulfillment of this hope may now have been thought to have been deferred to another time, or even to the world to come. The idea of a "book of remembrance," a record of the faithful, appears to have been an important topic in so-called apocalyptic writings (beside Dan. 12:1 see 7:10; 10:21; Rev. 3:5; 17:8; 20:12). Perhaps the "tablets of fate" (*ANET*, 541) or the "book of memorable deeds" (Est. 6:1) gave rise to the idea of a "book of life" (cf. also Ps. 139:16).

The reasons for being included in this "book of remembrance" are worth noting: "Those who feared the LORD and thought on his name" were included in the book. The "fear of the LORD" and the "name" were already important topics in 1:6. As opposed to that earlier instance, the "messenger" speaks here only in a positive manner of the "fear of the LORD" as an accomplished fact (see, e.g., Prov. 15:33; Ps. 128:4; Prov. 10:27; 14:27; 19:23).

17 Now the style changes still further—God speaks directly not to the people but about them. The language is solemn and uses profound traditional terminology: "LORD of hosts" (1 Sam. 4:4; see Mal. 3:12), "special possession" (Exod. 19:5; Deut. 7:6; 1 Pet. 2:9), "the day when I act" (Isa. 4:2; 24:21; 26:1; Jer. 31:31-34), "as a man who spares his son" (cf. e.g., Isa. 1:2; Deut. 8:5; 32:5-6).

The style of v. 17 comes close to that of eschatological predictions. The phrase "on the/that day" is used specifically in additions to earlier writings, and is intended to supplement these as an encouragement to readers (see, e.g., Isa. 10:20; 11:10, 11; 19:16ff.). Such language is seen often in later writings (see, e.g., Joel 3:1-3, 18; Zech. 13:1, 2; 14:1, 4, 6, 20). As distinct from earlier "day of Yahweh" words (e.g., in Amos 5:18-20), these encouraging words speak of God's act of salvation for the "remnant" (Isa. 10:20; 11:11), for Judah and Israel (19:16ff.), Judah and Jerusalem (Joel 3:1-3), the inhabitants of Jerusalem, the house of David (Zech. 13:1). Some passages make use of the same phrase, "day of Yahweh," to emphasize God's role "on that day" (Zech. 14:1-5, 9; Rev. 21:3-4). All of the above underlines God's love, mercy, and reacceptance of his people, who are described here as a "special possession" (see Exod. 19:5). This figure of speech can be illustrated by words dealing also with other nations, for example, Egypt and Assyria (Isa. 19:16-17, 18; 27:12-13). The phrase "as a man spares his son," another figure of speech, touches the theology of Isa. 40 – 55. There, attention is repeatedly drawn to the caring God, who does not want his people to suffer anymore (40:1-2; 43:1-7, 21; 49:15; etc.; see also Eph. 2:8-10).

18 This prediction goes right back to the center of the problem in vv. 14-15. Now the people are addressed directly: "Then once more you shall distinguish." But that will only happen "on the day when I act" (v. 17).

CHAPTER 4

THE SUN OF RIGHTEOUSNESS (4:1-3)

1 The punishment of "the arrogant and all evildoers" reminds one of 3:2, the description of the "day of the LORD," which will be a time of purification for "the sons of Levi" according to 3:2-3. This instance, however, speaks of it as a day of destruction: "(they) will be stubble; the day that comes shall burn them up" (cf. Amos 5:18-20; 1 Cor. 3:13-15).

The day of the LORD can probably be explained simply as being the time when God meets mankind and this world face to face. The fierce fire that "devours" and "consumes" is God himself (Exod. 24:17; Ps. 50:3; Deut. 4:24; Heb. 12:29). This figure of speech probably originated from ancient ideas of what the appearance of God was like. Such "theophanies" are occasionally mentioned (see, e.g., Exod. 3:2-6; 19:18; 33:3; Deut. 5:4; Ps. 97:2-5; Hab. 3:3-4; Rev. 1:14; cf. E. Jenni, "Day of the Lord," *IDB*, 1:784-85). However, such descriptions usually served to emphasize God's jealousy (e.g, Deut. 4:23-24; see 5:9; 6:15), his power to destroy the enemies threatening Israel (e.g., Deut. 9:3) or people who "reject the law of the LORD of hosts" (Isa. 5:24-25; 9:19; 10:16-17; 30:27-28; 33:14). This can be compared with "the lake of fire" in Rev. 20:11-15. Isaiah spoke of God and his glory as "fire." There may be an association with the temple and its altar (see 29:1-2 = "Ariel"; 31:9; cf. Gen. 15:17). Zechariah speaks of God's protection and glory in a similar way (2:5; cf. Isa. 4:5), reminding one of the "pillar of cloud . . . pillar of fire" (Exod. 13:21-22).

The last clause, "so that it will leave them neither root nor branch," is a variation on an ancient curse (cf. Amos 2:9; Hos. 9:16; Isa. 5:24). One of its earliest occurrences is in a Phoenician inscription (S. Gevirtz, "West-Semitic curses," *VT* 3 [1953] 149-50); another (in part) in an Ugaritic text (1 Aqhat III:53-54; *CML*, 64-65). Sometimes this saying is also used as a promise (see, e.g., Isa. 37:31). That such a curse was used at this point

111

can be explained simply by the fact that such curses were evidently in popular use at the time. They were used to describe total destruction.

2   As in 3:18 the people are again directly addressed: "you who fear my name." The figure of speech in the following sentence is interesting: "the sun of righteousness shall rise, *with healing in its wings*." It cannot be ruled out that this refers to the Egyptian representation of the sun with wings as a symbol of the creator-god Re. The frequent use of Egyptian ideas, texts, and symbols in the OT was due to the prolonged relationship between Egypt and Palestine. Sometimes this fact is given less weight in favor of the perhaps more obvious influence from Mesopotamia.

The two expressions in this figure of speech, "sun of righteousness" and "with healing in its wings," are good examples of the extent of Egyptian influence on people living in Palestine. The highest god in Egypt was the sun-god, although his name and cults changed several times. He was the creator, giver of life, father of the king, of mankind, and of all beings. He was also the judge. The last was most important to the Egyptians because of their belief in life after death. Expressions like "He uncovers the deeps out of darkness" (Job 12:22) and "God will bring every deed into judgment" (Eccl. 12:14) are based on this ancient conviction (cf. Ps. 19:6b; 1 Cor. 4:5; etc.).

The second expression, "with healing in its wings," alludes to the same god who blesses all he has created: the "wings" are the rays of the sun, sometimes depicted as arms and hands reaching down to earth (in a well-known picture from Ikhnaton's time; see *ANEP,* nos. 408, 409; cf. also no. 415). A hymn to Aton, the sun-god as Ikhnaton (actually Amen-hotep IV, ca. 1375-1357 B.C.) called him, shows many similarities to Ps. 104 (cf. *ANET,* 369-71). According to M. Dahood (*Psalms III,* Anchor Bible [Garden City, NY: Doubleday, 1970], 33) this psalm was influenced indirectly by Egyptian ideas "through Canaanite mediation, more specifically through Phoenician intervention" because of the latter's frequent contact with the Egyptians. In Israel such ideas were applied to Yahweh the God of Israel, as can be seen from Mal. 4:2; Ps. 104; and other passages. The "healing" is a revitalization (see Isa. 40:31). The symbolic expression "wings" is frequently found with the application to Yahweh, though independent of the "sun." This is probably due to another origin — perhaps from the "winged creatures" often depicted in Mesopotamia and mentioned in many OT passages (see, e.g., Exod. 25:20; Isa. 6:2; Ezek. 1:5-6). The "wings" of Yahweh are also used metaphorically to mean "protection" (see, e.g., Ps. 17:8; 36:7; Matt. 23:37; etc.) or "help" (Exod. 19:4; Deut. 32:11).

Early Christians took Mal. 4:2a to be a messianic prediction and applied it to Christ as savior. Rudolph points out (*Maleachi*, 289) that this title "sun of righteousness" was identified in Rome with *sol invictus*, whose birthday was on Dec. 25 — hence our date for Christmas Day. However, "the rising of the sun" is an imagery of healing and help, which is also used elsewhere in the Bible and may have still another root. The light of the sun, the sun itself, is a symbol for God (Ps. 19:1-6; Rev. 1:16). God's glory is seen as replacing the sun (Isa. 24:23). The phraseology normally applied to the sun is now being used for God and his glory (Isa. 60:1). This bright light of God's glory brings healing to his people (Isa. 35:1-2, 3-7). God's healing power is first referred to in the ancient "Song of Moses," Deut. 32:39 (see also Exod. 15:26). From the comments at Mal. 4:1 (on "theophanies") it may be possible to find a link to this picture in v. 2.

Verse 2b reminds us not only of Isa. 35:6 but also of 51:3, both of which speak of God mercifully comforting "Zion" and reviving his people. Here and throughout his book, Deutero-Isaiah speaks of God's compassion on his people, whom he plans to bring back from their exile into the land of their fathers. This will be a time of great joy (42:10; 44:23; 49:13). God's motivation for this new act of salvation is the same as for the first act of salvation in Moses' time — his "steadfast love," his faithfulness to the covenant (Exod. 3:6, 15-17; Deut. 4:37; 7:7-9; Isa. 54:10).

The NT celebrates still another act of God's merciful love and faithfulness: this is what the writers of the NT have understood Jesus to be. In many instances they use words and ideas originally found in the OT in order to describe and underline the acts of God through Jesus. When John the Baptist asked Jesus through two of his disciples, "Are you he who is to come?" (Matt. 11:3-5), Matthew used the words of Isa. 35:5-6 (cf. 29:18-19; 61:1) to describe what was happening through Jesus: God's love and healing had come, his glory had appeared for the people to see (cf. 35:2).

3 The "wicked" is the most direct identification of those who oppose God, and is found frequently throughout the Psalms and Proverbs (see, e.g., Ps. 1:1, 4-6). As far as the pious and the wise were concerned, the ruin of the "wicked" was certain and inevitable (Prov. 3:25). The pious ("the poor") themselves would witness this end (Isa. 26:6).

This prediction of the eventual rehabilitation of the pious, and of the shameful end of the "wicked" concludes the last message and dispute of Malachi. He refutes the suggestion that to serve God is meaningless. However, he reserves the final evidence of this for the day when God will act.

ELIJAH WILL COME! (4:4-6)

The remaining three verses of Malachi may be regarded as the concluding postscript by the editor of the whole collection of the prophetic books. On the one hand, it serves as a last reminder to his readers of what was, according to this editor, the whole purpose of the prophets (v. 4). On the other hand, it expresses an expectation that once the time of the prophets comes to an end, God will send still one more prophet; he will be like the first of the prophets, Moses. He will then bring about the great return to God (v. 5). With this promise he obviously reminds the readers of the prediction in Deut. 18:15: "The LORD your God will raise up for you a prophet like me . . . him you shall heed."

4 The word "law" in the RSV here represents Heb. *torah*, as we found in 2:6-9. In the same sense it is also used in Leviticus, Numbers, Deuteronomy, Psalms, and Proverbs. This means that "Torah" refers to the collection of instructions which is contained in "the five books of Moses." The earlier prophets (Amos, Hosea, Micah, Isaiah [chs. 1 – 33], Jeremiah, and Ezekiel) do not use the term "Torah" very often. But many of their messages and critiques refer directly to instructions and demands contained in the Torah (see above at 3:5; cf. further Exod. 22:22; Deut. 24:17-18; Hos. 4:1-2; Amos 2:6b, 7a; 5:14-15; etc.). Jesus and his contemporaries used this word in the same sense (see, e.g., Matt. 5:17-18; Luke 16:16-17).

5 This specific prediction of the coming of "Elijah" is usually considered to be the earliest statement of its kind. The three Synoptic Gospels refer to it as the teaching of the "scribes" (Mark 9:11-13, par.) i.e., the biblical scholars of that time; yet there is an important difference between this NT reference and Mal. 4:5-6. In the NT "Elijah" is definitely the forerunner of the Messiah, while in Malachi "Elijah" himself is the Messiah who makes the people turn to God once more. He will thus save them from the "curse," because the "day of Yahweh" will be both salvation and condemnation (see 3:2; 4:1; cf. S. Szikszai, "Elijah the Prophet," *IDB*, 2:90).

From this particular example we can see once again how the writers of the NT made use of the OT. Sometimes people think that it was "wrong" to use OT words and ideas for the purpose of describing, or even "proving," events and convictions of people who lived much later, as is the case here. But everything must be considered and judged in the light of the standards and customs of the people living at the time in question. The practice of Jewish rabbinical teaching of that period (ca. 1st cent. B.C. and 1st cent. A.D.) is evident here (cf. e.g., G. Vermes, *Jesus the Jew*, 150-51). People at that time did not think in historical categories as we are taught to do today. Times, symbols, and events could easily be taken from one period and applied to another.

In this manner, Matthew used the word "son" from Hos. 11:1b and applied it to Jesus (2:15), but it would be unfair to accuse Matthew of having done so superficially. Behind this new application we can recognize a completely new theological insight: the "son" in Hos. 11:1 was, of course, Israel, the people of God. According to the theological understanding of the early Church, Jesus was the founder of the new people of God just as much as Jacob/Israel had been the father of the old. The old Israel came out of Egypt by God's mighty hand. In the same way, so this story wants to tell us, God also saved Jesus (i.e., the one who represents the new people of God) from Egypt and brought him out again, back to "the land of Israel" (Matt. 2:21). Similar symbolic applications of OT words and ideas may be found in many NT passages (see, e.g., 1 Cor. 3:16-17; 10:4; 15:45; Heb. 9:11-12; 1 Pet. 2:4-6; cf. Matt. 21:42).

6 The last verse in this postscript emphasizes "return": it is to be a real process of correcting attitudes, renewing relationships, and of "doing," not just of "speaking." "Return" is demanded in numerous passages throughout both the OT and the NT. Mal. 3:7 formulates it as an invitation in terms similar to those used in Jer. 4:1. It is quite obvious, however, that Mal. 4:6 intends to refute the possible misunderstanding of "return" as a kind of "spiritual exercise," so it emphasizes that "return" must be realized in renewed living in this same old world. Only this will prevent the "curse" from coming upon the people.

The NT equivalent of "return" is translated in the RSV as "repent." One interesting instance is in Luke 16:27-31. In content and in intention this passage exactly echoes the concern of Malachi (e.g., 3:7). The Torah pays specific attention to the relationships of children to their parents, and also vice versa, not only because of Exod. 20:12 (par.) but more particularly because of the responsibility of the parents to teach their children, "lest you forget" (see, e.g, Deut. 4:9-10; 6:7, 20-25; 31:12-13).

The curse in v. 6 is explained by the RSV mg in terms of a "ban of utter destruction" (Heb. *herem*). This is an ancient technical term of "holy war" meaning the total "devotion" of human beings, animals, and possessions to God (see, e.g., Lev. 27:20-21, 28-29; Num. 21:2-3; Josh. 6:18). Such a "ban" is also to be a punishment for those who worship "other gods" (see, e.g., Exod. 22:20; Deut. 7:25-26).

CONCLUSION

In some versions of the Bible the book of Malachi is the last book of the OT. This may suggest to the reader that the OT links smoothly with the NT, especially with its first book, the Gospel of Matthew (see Mal. 4:5-6, Matt. 17:11). However, this impression would be a deception. The order of books in the Hebrew Bible is very different. It is in three main groups: (1) Torah (Genesis through Deuteronomy); (2) the Prophets ("earlier": Joshua, Judges, and 1 Samuel through 2 Kings; "later": Isaiah, Jeremiah, Ezekiel, and the "Twelve"); (3) the Writings (all the rest, including Daniel and ending with 2 Chronicles).

The "Christian" order of the books of the OT is the result of a process that began about the time the LXX came into being (3rd to 2nd cent. B.C.) and continued over a long time. In fact, the order of the books in the Protestant Bibles of today dates from the time of the Reformation. In Roman Catholic editions of the Bible a number of books are included which are otherwise found only in the LXX. These are commonly called the "Apocrypha" (from the Greek *apokryphos*, "hidden"). Some of these are placed in such a way as to separate the OT from the NT. This fact, among others, serves to remind the reader of the complicated history of the Bible, but of course also of the soil out of which our Christian faith was able to grow. Our God, the LORD of the OT, is not just the one who made himself known to his people in OT times. He is the God who later made himself known once again in NT times, through Jesus of Nazareth.

The books which separate the OT from the NT are the fruits of the faith, labor, and sufferings of the Jews. God's people did not simply die in exile. Nor did they (equally simply) continue to exist right into NT times. During and after the Exile of 587 B.C. a process of preservation, transformation, and renewal took place. This process marks the beginning of Judaism. The fruits of this process may be found in the biblical books dated after Deutero-Isaiah, right through to Haggai, Zechariah, Nehemiah,

117

Ezra, and Malachi. The progress of Judaism is reflected in other writings, for example, the Apocrypha and the NT. Yet faith was mostly lived, not written down. These people cheerfully placed their hope in the care of the faithful and loving God of their fathers, in the care of him who promised not to forsake those who trust in him.

Commitment to a tradition nourishes a community, but when such commitment excludes other ways of thinking and acting, it creates conflict. Tradition as a contributor to conflict may be seen in Judaism itself. Further, the tension between Jesus and these sects had its root in commitment to certain traditions. However, Jesus himself was a Jew, and so were his early followers, including Paul. Many traditions, words, parables, and stories in the NT of and about Jesus bear the mark of his Jewish origin. G. Vermes's book, *Jesus the Jew,* can be an eye-opener on many details in this respect. Nevertheless, Jesus' followers founded the Christian Church. In him, they recognized God's revelation, his act of salvation. To them the OT was fulfilled in Jesus' coming. That God acted through Jesus is expressed in the confession that Jesus is the "Christ," God's anointed king. This remains the faith of Christians to the present day.

Looking at the history of faith from this perspective, we may become joyfully aware of these continuing experiences with God. The roots of faith, reaching back to earliest times, can inspire us today. The God of the past is the God of the present. He continues to invite people to turn to him. This means seeking the meaning of life by living his love in such a way that all people, especially the poor, the oppressed, the suffering, and the sorrowful, can receive the life he wills for us all.

BIBLIOGRAPHY

Texts

Buber, M. *Die Fünf Bcher der Weisung*. 3rd ed. (Köln & Olten: Jakob Hegner, 1956).

Driver, G. R. *Canaanite Myths and Legends*. Old Testament Studies No. 3 (Edinburgh: T. & T. Clark, 1956).

Elliger, K., ed. *Maleachi*. In *Biblia Hebraica Stuttgartensia* (Stuttgart: Deutsche Bibelstiftung, 1977).

Kautzsch, E. *Die Pseudepigraphen des Alten Testaments* (Tübingen: Mohr, 1900).

Pritchard, J. B., ed. *Ancient Near Eastern Texts Relating to the Old Testament*. 3rd ed. (Princeton: Princeton University Press, 1969).

Vermes, G. *The Dead Sea Scrolls* (Harmondsworth: Penguin, 1973).

Books

Elliger, K. *Die Propheten: Nahum, Habakuk, Zephanja, Haggai, Sacharja, Maleachi*. Das Alte Testament Deutsch. 3rd ed. (Göttingen: Vandenhoek & Ruprecht, 1956).

Gray, J. *The Legacy of Canaan*. 2nd ed. Supplements to *Vetus Testamentum* 5 (Leiden: Brill, 1965).

Hengel, M. *Judaism and Hellenism*. Trans. J. Bowden. 2 vols. (London: SCM and Philadelphia: Fortress, 1974).

Knight, G. A. F. *The New Israel: Isaiah 56 – 66*. International Theological Commentary (Grand Rapids: Eerdmans and Edinburgh: Handsel, 1985).

Rudolph, W. *Haggai —Sacharja —Maleachi*. Kommentar zum Alten Testament (Gütersloh: Gütersloher Verlagshaus Gerd Mohn, 1976).

Verhoef, P. A. *The Books of Haggai and Malachi*. New International Commentary on the Old Testament (Grand Rapids: Eerdmans, 1987).

Vermes, G. *Jesus the Jew: A Historian's Reading of the Gospels* (London: Collins, 1973; repr. Philadelphia: Fortress, 1981).

Articles

Abba, R. "Priests and Levites." In *Interpreter's Dictionary of the Bible*. Ed. G. A. Buttrick, et al. (Nashville: Abingdon, 1962) 3:885.

Freedman, D. N., and Willoughby, B. E., *"mal''ak."* In *Theologisches Wörterbuch zum Alten Testament.* Ed. G. J. Botterweck, H. Ringgren, H.-J. Fabry (Stuttgart, Berlin, Köln, Mainz: Kohlhammer, 1984) 4:887ff.

Gevirtz, S. "West-Semitic curses and the problem of the origins of Hebrew law," *Vetus Testamentum* 11 (1961) 137-58.

Jenni, E. "Day of the Lord." In *Interpreter's Dictionary of the Bible.* Ed. G. A. Buttrick, et al. (Nashville: Abingdon, 1962) 1:784-85.

Saebo, M. *"yom."* In *Theologisches Wörterbuch zum Alten Testament.* Ed. G. J. Botterweck, H. Ringgren, H.-J. Fabry (Stuttgart, Berlin, Köln, Mainz: Kohlhammer, 1982) 3:583-84.

Szikszai, S. "Elijah the Prophet." In *Interpreter's Dictionary of the Bible.* Ed. G. A. Buttrick, et al. (Nashville: Abingdon, 1962) 2:88-90.